The Letter Box

An Entire Year of Illustrated Letters
WENDY DEWAR HUGHES

The Letter Box

An Entire Year of Illustrated Letters
WENDY DEWAR HUGHES

Summer Bay Press

The Letter Box

Copyright © 2018 Wendy Dewar Hughes

Published by Summer Bay Press
#14 – 1884 Heath Road, Agassiz, B.C. Canada V0M 1A2

www.wendydewarhughes.com

ISBN: 978-1-927626-85-6

All art and designs by Wendy Dewar Hughes
Cover design by Wendy Dewar Hughes

All rights reserved. No part of this publication may be reproduced, stored in a retrieval system, or transmitted in any form or by any means including electronic, mechanical, digital, photocopy, recording, or any other means without the prior permission of the author, except by a reviewer who may quote brief passages in a review. For permission contact:

Summer Bay Press
sumbay@telus.net

For my daughter, Olivia, who coloured on the walls too.

Happy New Year!

January can almost be described as the best of times and the worst of times, to reference Charles Dickens. It is the worst because it holds some of the darkest and coldest days of the year, particularly if you live in northern latitudes, and the best because January is a month of new beginnings.

Once the excitement, parties, and general hubbub that leads up to and includes the Christmas season has settled down and is behind us, we are suddenly presented with a brand new year to start fresh. In spite of winter's chill, a new year brings new hope.

Winter has its own special characteristics and offers chances to enjoy the snow and ice with outdoor sports like skiing and skating, or events such as winter carnivals.

Staying indoors can feel a little like hibernating, which is a wonderful concept to adopt for a while. There are few sights that compare with sunlight slanting across sparkling snow, or of trees wreathed in ice and looking for all the world like they're made of glass. Evergreens that belong on Christmas cards may be just out your window. When it's really cold, the snow crunches underfoot and frost collects on your eyelashes and nostrils. Believe me, if you haven't experienced this, it feels strange.

One of the best features of January is having a cozy house with a good furnace and big windows from which to view winter. The bird feeder is a-flutter with hungry winged friends for whom this location is "going south". The chickadees are my favourites; they're so cheeky and tame.

January is also a great month for reading good books and drinking hot chocolate. And eating all the chocolates left over from Christmas. (Are chocolates ever left over after New Year's? I think not.) I'm convinced that chocolate helps you get through tough times, and dearie, the middle of January can definitely qualify as a tough time in my book.

Have you noticed that department or grocery stores suddenly have huge displays of big tropical plants in January? They know what this month is about. It's so tempting to fill the house with flora when you can't go to sunnier climates, but since I already have enough plants (bought in previous January slumps) it's just nice to see all that greenery and dream a little.

While the snow falls and the wind blows, it's a great time to cozy up with a cup of tea (or hot chocolate) and a journal. Take a quiet look at the past year. Rather than look at your accomplishments right now, think about what gave you joy. What made you happy?

Answer these questions for yourself:
What made you laugh?
Where did you go that you enjoyed the most?
What activities were the most fun?
Whose company did you enjoy?
What day of the week and time of day is your favourite? Why?

There are good reasons to focus on joy, even in the midst of sorrow or difficulty. For one thing, it keeps you from sinking into an emotional quagmire. By that I mean any number of emotions that can take you lower. Let's not go there.

Now, remember the goals you made this time last year? How did they work out?

Sometimes life takes turns that we can neither predict nor avoid. Someone close to you passes away, you have health issues to deal with, the economy tanks—it could be anything but it veers you right off track. Or maybe an opportunity comes along that is irresistible. Or perhaps you just changed your mind about the plans you had. It happens, and it's okay.

When you look back on your year, what accomplishment are you most proud of? Is there anything that you want to continue or to grow?

Bringing those successes forward establishes a platform for launching your new year. So when you put all your goodies from the previous year together, what does it indicate?

Pivot 180° now and instead of looking backward, let's look forward. There is much to be gained from looking at where we've been, but if you're always looking backward, you can't move forward.

I've found in my own life that when difficulty has marked a period of time it's like it has left a scar on my soul and continues to make itself felt. Often there is pain involved and of course, it's important to take the time you need to heal, but dwelling in that place doesn't get you out of it.

Take a tip from Scarlet O'Hara, the plucky heroine from the novel and movie, Gone With The Wind. When things got tough, our Scarlet made the decision not to think about that today, but to think about it tomorrow instead.

So when memories that trouble you come back to haunt, you can always make the decision not to think about them. Replace the space in your thoughts with something positive and pro-active.

All right, now let's look at what this new year might bring in light of your joy list.

One of the best ways to visualize what you want to happen in the year ahead is to create a vision board. This is quick and simple and requires only a big piece of Bristol board, a pair of scissors and a glue stick, and a pile of old magazines or catalogues.

I always want to plan in travel, so I pick up travel brochures from local agencies to use for my planning.

To create your board, simply cut out images from your magazines that fit with your year's plans and glue them to the board. When you hang it up in a place you will see it frequently, it will keep your dreams top of mind.

If you like, make notes on your vision board alongside the pictures. You can add a date when you would like to have each item come true, or note how you expect to feel when you've achieved each dream. It's very inspiring.

So what are those dreams, hopes, and wishes? Only you can answer that for yourself. Take some time to write a list of everything you'd love to be, have, or do this year. Don't edit the list, or talk yourself out of whatever you want even before you write it down. Just write everything down.

Next, you will want to prioritize the list in order of importance or how passionate you are about each item. Once you've decided on those items, you'll need to break them down into steps you can take to achieve the dream.

It's not as complicated as it might sound. Start with the big things then break them down into smaller steps.

We are fortunate, living at this time and wherever you live. We have choices and options. We have opportunities denied to many and unavailable at other times in history.

I believe that for each of us our main calling, if you will, is to be the best you that you can be. That means not trying to be anyone other than who you really are at your most YOU.

The trick to living the life you want is first being real about what you truly want. Once you're clear on that, it's much easier to shed what doesn't fit. It's like a painting where you include only the right elements.

That gives us both a lot to think about going into the year.

Happy planning!

Wendy

Hello, hello,

February doesn't always deliver up many nice days in my corner of the continent. My least favourite season is winter, and these winter weeks sometimes seem to each last for months.

Where I live in a village in British Columbia, winter hit hard this year with heavy snow, freezing temperatures, harsh winds, and dark days. One of the reasons we moved to this area near the west coast many years ago was to escape Canada's deep freeze winters that occur on the east side of the Rocky Mountains. Often we don't have snow all winter, just rain, but this year was an exception.

I went out for a walk today and though the sky is dove grey and the trees still skeletal, there are signs of spring if you look closely. The local lumber store has wheelbarrows, shiny with bright paint, out front, along with a rack of garden tools.

The rhododendrons already have their buds set, and I saw the first tiny shoots on iris rhizomes in the community gardens behind where I live. I love to go walking amongst the beds there and watch the gardens progress. There is still snow on the ground here and there, in dirty clumps now, but the mountain I see from my window is still white far down its slopes.

There is a certain hint of spring

My mom passed away a few weeks ago after a short illness. She was 85 and had been strong and healthy all her life but she fell and broke her arm, then followed that up with three heart attacks in four days. It was all too much for her heart to recover its former strength and she continued to decline.

We buried her on the Canadian prairies where she had spent her entire life and in the land that she loved. I'm missing her as I write this. She was one of those "just get on with it" pragmatic farm people and never complained much about anything.

My mom was amazingly creative. As an accomplished seamstress, her sewing room overflows with projects yet to be started or completed. It's like she stepped away from her sewing machine and just never got back to that project.

I'm so thankful for inheriting her can-do attitude toward life, yet as a creative person doing creative work, I still find that sometimes it's hard to stay inspired. I wish that I leapt out of bed every day filled with enthusiasm. It's not always so.

I never find myself short of ideas, in fact, I have books full of notes, and cupboards full of projects to work on. However, sometimes I lack the actual motivation to do anything with them.

I'm a practical person and when things don't work like they are supposed to, I want to know why so I can fix what's wrong. So when I find myself unmotivated to do the work that I know I love to do, there has to be a reason, or reasons, why.

You may find yourself in the same situation. Procrastination is the bane of many a creative person. We want to do those lovely, exciting projects, but can't seem to get them started. Or we start but can't get past what I call "the ugly middle" (more about this later), and the enthusiasm withers away like an unwatered plant.

It's not enough to shrug and accept that you're a procrastinator. What an awful thought anyway! Don't give yourself that label unless you want to be stuck there—and you don't.

I've never had a big problem with procrastination but sometimes I just don't want to get up and do the work. The thing is, there is always a valid reason. The trick is to ascertain what that reason is.

Someone I know struggles with putting things off. When we talked about it, he realized that rather than looking at the next step, he saw the enormity of the project and froze. My reasons are completely different.

Here is a list I've come up with to explain why we can all run out of juice for creative projects. You may see yourself here, (or not).

1. Too much to do. Sometimes I'm pulled in so many directions at once that I can barely move. I may have a book to work on, or a painting, yet I can't concentrate on it long enough to move it forward.

2. Too tired. I'll be honest. Sometimes I don't sleep very well. I tend to internalize stresses and they come back to haunt me as a busy mind at night. It's hard to be motivated when you're feeling exhausted or drained.

3. Emotional disequilibrium. When something emotional is bothering me, it has the same effect on my ability to be creative as having a crying child pulling at my pant leg.

4. Constant interruptions. The phone won't stop ringing. Clients want one more thing; too many commitments on too many days of the week. These all make it hard to allow my creative side to come out and play.

5. Self-doubt. Oh, big ouch! Being assailed by thoughts like, "Why do I bother?" or "Who do I think I am to try this?" will derail creative motivation faster than a fire hose can douse a candle flame.

6. Not knowing my next step. When I don't know what the next move is, it's hard to motivate myself to make it. It's like staring into a dark room and feeling around for the light switch.

How can you fly when you don't know where to go?

You can probably think of a few more ways that creativity or forward movement is compromised and motivation gets siphoned off. I've got some creative suggestions for getting back in the go-for-it mood.

So, what to do?

I've managed to do a lot of creative projects over the course of my life and career (if you can call it that), so I'm no stranger to bumping up against lack of motivation. The reason that I've been able to persevere in the face of discouragement is that I've learned to identify the cause of it and take steps to deal with the root problem.

Here is what I do:

Ask where the malaise originates. Am I too tired? Am I overwhelmed with other work? Do I have some emotional issue on my mind that I need to deal with? Am I feeling hopeless, and wondering if I'll ever succeed?

I ask myself, what CAN I do?

Once I know the source of my current condition, I can take steps to correct it. This might come in the form of taking a nap, or spreading my client workload out over a longer period.

Sometimes what I need most is fresh air and exercise, and simply going for a walk does the job.

I also ask myself, what CAN I do? There is usually at least one step I can take in the direction I want to go, so rather than looking at the big picture, I look for the next baby step. This frequently opens my eyes to the step after that, and the one after that one.

If I am feeling like what I'm doing is pointless, I need to examine my reason for doing it at all. If I don't even want to do this thing, I need to do something else.

The thing is, creative work has the wonderful distinction of being not only a means to an end but also an end in itself. The very act of doing something creative produces something besides the finished work: a sense of fulfillment.

I'm going to do some painting now. I've made it a goal to work on something arty every day. It might be a pencil sketch, or a watercolour, or just a list of ideas but having made the decision, it's now part of my daily plan.

The same system works for me when I write. In order to accomplish the work, it has to be on my calendar and be part of my daily plan. It's amazing how much you can get done just by chipping away at the project. And knowing that I have an appointment with a paintbrush, or a manuscript, helps a lot when inspiration wanes, or when the project looks pathetic at the "ugly" halfway point.

The trick is to keep on going. Just don't stop. We'll all get there, motivated or not.

Love and hugs,
Wendy

Fabulous February

Hello, Sweet friend,

Little indications of the end of winter are starting to appear around here. When I left the airport after arriving home from my family farm in Saskatchewan, I saw a bush just opening up its first pink blossoms. Oh, delight!

The surprising thing about my trip east to the prairies is that the weather there was bright, clear, and unseasonably warm. The snow that covered the landscape vanished in a couple of days. That produced a lot of farm mud but the warmth was definitely welcome.

> Grief is the price we pay for love.
> Queen Elizabeth II

This month has been unexpectedly busy. If you know me, you'll know that I'm not a fan of being overly busy. The concept that busy equals personal value doesn't wash with me. There are no prizes going to those who can brag about being busier than everyone else.

My mom passed away in January and I am one of the executors on her will. Although it's not proving to be as daunting as it sounds, there are still time-consuming jobs that need to be done to make sure everything is accomplished.

My siblings and I have inherited the farm that has been in our family for more than 100 years. That includes cleaning out a house that my parents lived in since I was a child. It's a big home with lots of rooms. My dad was an accomplished builder and created plenty of storage spaces.

My mom had a wide variety of creative interests and went for it every time she took up a new hobby or occupation. All that storage space is full of her materials for her interests. I went to the prairies with my sister and my sister-in-law, and boy, did we ever do a lot of work. There wasn't much Mom threw out over the years.

It's already two months into the year and I've decided to make some predictions. You might think that it's a little late to get started on this project but stay with me.

I predict that you'll get whatever you believe you can have and what you decide to go after. I know from my own experience that this works. You can't have one without the other.

You get to choose what your life is going to look like. I'm not suggesting that you can snap your fingers and every one of your dreams will come true. We're grown-ups so we know that fantasy is not going to work.

Sunrise on the prairie

The first thing you have to do is decide what you want. It can be anything—simple and small, or large and complicated. Perhaps you want to learn to knit or speak a foreign language. You'll need to make up your mind that it's a goal.

Set a deadline for when you want to achieve this goal. If you want to fly to Europe for a holiday, you have to decide when you want to go.

Then you need to make a plan. In my program, The Wish Plan, I go into depth on how to do this, but the method is so easy to do, you can create your plan in less than an hour.

The more we love the better we are.
Jeremy Taylor

My next prediction for the year is that we will all be as healthy as we decide to be. Again, nothing magical here. If you decide to take steps to become healthier, the chances are very good that you will.

Full disclosure, I suffered from adrenal fatigue for nearly eight years. Lots of things went wrong in my body as a result of several emotional and physical blows. I gained a bunch of weight (mostly as medication side-effects) and nothing I tried made it shift. It was more important to me at the time to deal with the underlying conditions and get healthy rather than put more stress on my body by trying to make drastic changes to my diet.

Finally, I felt in a position to lose some weight and become fitter. After recovering from adrenal fatigue, I discovered that my thyroid was low and weight had piled on as a result of my sluggish metabolism. Once that condition came to light and I was able to address it, the weight gain stopped. I started to lose on a sensible system with some good products and diet changes. It feels good.

I predict that if you make small changes in your diet and physical fitness habits, you will be healthier too. One of my strategies is to cut out sugar. Another is to take a walk outside every day.

I predict that more sunshine will make you feel better, as will more sleep.

Cutting out activities that don't give you joy will lift your heart and give you energy for what you love.

Removing items that are no longer useful from your home will give you more peace. These are all simple moves and changes that I predict will make for a happier year.

Loss and change

It struck me when my mom passed away into her eternity with the Lord, that my life had suddenly changed. Not only had I lost one of my best friends on earth but now I was also without parents. You never really anticipate this condition if your parents live to a good age.

It's a big loss, and with it changes come. The problem with losses is that we can get stuck there and dwell on our grief. When sadness enters our days, it can soon take over. The unfortunate part is that when given too much space in our hearts, it will move in and take over. Sadness interrupts your destiny.

How then do you avoid sadness and grief from invading your soul?

Sadness is understandable, but also it's about you. The way out is to look forward rather than back, outward rather than inward.

My mother lived a long, good life. She was the kind of person who when she made a decision, she never wavered. She trusted God all the days of her life. She seldom complained about her situation even when life got difficult. And at times, it certainly did.

There are lessons to be gleaned from these attitudes. Making the best of a loss turns it into a positive experience. There is always good in every situation. We just have to look for it. As much as I love and miss my parents, a chapter in my life has ended and a new one has begun.

Change your thoughts and you change your world.

Norman Vincent Peal

Experiencing losses and changes of any kind is part of life. When things happen, people will often tell you that "life goes on". Sometimes it's the last thing you want to hear when it seems like your own world has stopped turning.

Know that it will get easier, that there are people who love you, and don't be afraid to ask for help if you need it.

Love and hugs,
Wendy

Hello my dears,

Where I live, spring is calculated by the appearance or disappearance of birds. They seem to know what the weather and climate are going to do far more than we humans do, regardless of modern tracking systems.

A few weeks ago, I saw the first robin in my neighbourhood. And the Collared Eurasian doves started cooing again last week. I don't know where they've been all winter but I assume they went south. Smart birds.

However, spring is clearly not all the way here because there are still swans in the fields. They overwinter in our area and go north in the summer. So, if they're still here in mid-March, that's an indication that winter is still hanging on. Needless to say, I'm looking forward to the day when they've gone again, not that they're not a joy to see, but that they signal a turning of the seasons.

> *The most simple things can bring the most happiness.*
> — ISABELLA SCORUPCO

Out my window, through the pouring rain this morning, I saw one tiny yellow blob on the forsythia bush in my yard. Really, I had to squint to see it but realized that it was a blossom, the first one to open on the entire tree. Yay! That's a sure sign of spring around here.

Speaking of opening...

...this morning I opened my bedroom closet door and thought, "What don't I like here anymore? Is there anything I would miss if I got rid of it?"

In the spirit of simplifying—the theme this month—asking those questions help me decide what to eliminate. We all love our favourite things, and we should probably keep them if they give us joy. But that can add up to too much stuff that we don't use, for a variety of reasons.

I use a simple mental checklist for deciding whether to keep garments. You're welcome to use it on your own closet.

- Do I love it?
- Does it fit me well?
- Does it make me look thinner? (This is just me. Your goal might be different.)
- Does it cover well, or will bending over result in a cleavage-show, or some other kind of show that I don't want?
- Does it work with at least three other things in the closet?
- Does it hide what I want it to hide?
- Does the colour flatter me? (Good-bye yellows and browns.)
- Do I feel wonderful when I wear it?
- Does it remind me of a memory that I want—or don't want?
- Am I okay with the care it requires?

If you wear clothes that don't suit you, you're a fashion victim. You have to wear clothes that make you look better.

— VIVIENNE WESTWOOD

I have a long, navy, light wool sweater that has been in my closet for probably thirty years. It's a classic style, makes me look thinner, and works with all kinds of things in the closet. It's a keeper and never shows wear.

Recently, I eliminated a pretty pink shell top from my closet. While I loved the colour and the sparkly bits across the front, it was so low that I found myself always tossing the straps back over my shoulders so it wouldn't be cleavage city. The fabric, rayon knit with spandex, which I love, also rested across my middle so as to glorify the roadmap of stretch marks that I received when pregnant with a nine-pound baby.

While the colour was perfect and the care was easy, it didn't pass on the cover/hide aspect. I blessed someone else with it.

A striped, long-sleeved T-shirt met the same fate. Why? It was too short. Everything else worked except that one aspect. Now a shorter person can enjoy it.

Seasonal changes are great times for closet clean-outs. They are also good times to review how you want the next quarter of the year to go.

> *I believe in comfort. If you don't feel comfortable in your clothes, it's hard to think of anything else.*
> — DONNA KARAN

> *It's good to have plans and dreams, but don't be surprised if God brings you somewhere else.*
> — ANNE F. BEILER

Not having a strategy for my near future has been unsettling, so I've focussed on simplifying in order to re-gain my equilibrium.

Surprisingly, it has helped a lot. I can give my attention to something concrete that will result in good things happening.

Simplifying your life is not only about simplifying your surroundings. Sure, you can attack the garage or the front hall closet and you'll undoubtedly feel better for having done it. But simplifying how you spend your time is possibly even more valuable.

With today's technology and social media "opportunities" we can all become experts at time frittering. After all, people post cool stuff on Facebook and Pinterest. If I'm being honest with myself, spending hours on these pursuits (yours might be different—computer games anyone?) is not the best use of my time in light of where I want my life to go.

This is a big subject so suffice to say, if it's not leading you in the direction of your wishes and dreams, perhaps you need to re-think spending your precious life's minutes and hours on it.

Happy Spring!

Wendy

> *Follow your dreams, believe in yourself and don't give up.*
> — RACHAEL CORRIE

Dear Beautiful You,

I've been thinking a lot this week about socks. I'm not especially fond of socks, not for what they are, but for what they represent.

I wear socks only when it's cold enough for my feet to be uncomfortable without them. I much prefer going barefoot so having to wear socks means that it's cold out. As someone who is perpetually chilly (low thyroid will do that) I want it warm all the time.

Alas, we don't always get what we want and this winter has been a long, cold, wet one here on Canada's west coast. Signs of spring are appearing but barefoot weather is not yet in sight.

But listen, no matter how you may be affected by your environment, and we all are whether we recognize it or not, we can always find something for which to be thankful.

Forsythia blooming in my yard.

I'll admit, cloudy weather that goes on for weeks gets me down. It's work to stay upbeat when you want to crawl back in bed with a good book and stay there until the sun shines again.

(Okay, I often feel like spending the day in bed with a good book anyway. There are so many great books to read.)

I find that the more I focus on the miserable climate conditions, the worse I feel about them. It doesn't help that my husband is a weather watcher. He's got all the gadgets and has even recorded the weather in a diary for going on fifteen years.

In the face of this, it's important to choose something else to fix my focus on.

Keep your face to the sunshine and you can never see the shadow.
— Helen Keller

This habit works equally well for other adversities or misadventures that come our way. We like to think that we're in control of our lives but, pfffft!

That's not entirely true. We're in control of some things, sure, but there is plenty that we can do nothing about.

When stuff happens that we can't change, we have choices. We do tend to forget that we can always choose our response to events. No one can tell us how to think or feel. We get to decide that for ourselves.

Rather than trying not to think about the pain in my shoulder, the unrelenting rain, or the fact that the landlord just cut down all of my heirloom rose bushes, I'm deciding to focus on something else. Trying not to think about something is still thinking about it.

Here's a quick list of possibilities:

- Plan a vacation
- Go for coffee with a friend
- Choose patterns and fabric to sew something
- Clean your office (and does mine ever need it!)
- Update the spice cupboard
- Read a new novel
- Movie binge on a theme, i.e. historical period, 1950s films, favourite actor
- Catch up on a job you've put off
- Summer wardrobe shop
- Paint a picture
- Count your blessings

Basically, look for something that makes you happy. Do you need to take a step back and look at your emotional state objectively? If someone else were to examine you, what would he or she report?

In my case, I think the observer would say to me: "This person has had a hard winter and needs something to cheer her up."

So that's what I've done. I realized that in the midst of this "dismalia" (I made that word up) when I really need two weeks on a beach but can't go right now, a little cheering up will help. I asked myself what would do that for me?

> "Consciously controlling your thoughts is not just the first step in this process; it is the main step."
> — DR. CAROLINE LEAF

When you're feeling blue, it can be difficult to come up with creative thoughts or ideas. Helen Keller, who was rendered blind, deaf, and dumb by disease as a small child, famously said, "Keep your face to the sunshine and you can never see the shadow." Her reference to sunshine and shadow are metaphorical but the idea works.

If I keep my focus on what gives me joy, or cheers me up, I won't have time to dwell on what gets me down. According to Dr. Caroline Leaf in her book, Who Switched off My Brain—Controlling Toxic Thoughts and Emotions, negative thoughts actually cause damage to the brain!

I highly recommend everything by Dr. Leaf, and have to admit that learning about the damaging consequences of negativity is sobering indeed. Even when you have plenty about which to be miserable, do yourself a favour and think good thoughts.

Always remember, you are enough just as you are. You have the power to change how and what you think, and therefore change the course of your life. How fabulous is that!

Until next time,

Hello, my dear,

Sometime last year I listened to Martha Stewart's book, The Martha Rules, on CD in my car while driving. Martha herself narrated it. I thought that since she's had a great deal of business success, I might learn something from her, which I did.

Her most famous statement is, "It's a good thing," and I was surprised to discover that her goal and purpose in everything she does, according to her, is to make good things for people to help them live good lives.

While I wouldn't call myself a fan, since I've never seen Martha Stewart's television shows, I do admire her motivation and everything she has created. What impressed me about Martha Stewart was not her ability to clean a house, put on a wedding, or write a cookbook. It was that she had a vision for what she wanted to create. In the process of listening to the story of how she built her business, I learned some things—about business, not about cakes.

I'm sure from time to time we've all asked ourselves what our purpose in life is. I believe that there is an overarching purpose for all of us, that is, as Jesus said, to love God with all your heart, soul, and strength, and love your neighbour as you love yourself.

It's all about love.

These are pretty good words to live by. It's worth noting that all the instructions are about love.

At different times in life, your purpose will be different. Such as, when I was the mother of young children, my purpose was loving and caring for them as they grew. (At times it was also just getting a good night's sleep but that's another story.)

As my children grew up, my purpose was to prepare them to be independent adults ready to make their own way in the world. Sometimes my main focus has been to feel better and become healthier. At other times, it has been to learn something new to further a personal or business goal.

My idea for the Letter Box was primarily to create a way to share good thoughts, ideas, joy, fun, and inspiration. The world will tell us that there is something wrong with us, that our lives aren't complete unless we buy a product, or that everyone else has it better.

But we have the power to decide how we feel, regardless of what anyone says. Brain science, a fascinating topic, has discovered how thoughts are formed and where feelings come from.

Sometimes the enemy can be our own thoughts.

JOEL OSTEEN

Basically, thoughts we think become beliefs and feelings follow those beliefs. For example, if as a child you see your mother freak out at the sight of a mouse, you'll think that mice are frightful. The belief you'll adopt will be that when you see a mouse, you should scream and leap up on the nearest chair.

The feeling that follows is anywhere from startle to full-on phobia. However, if like my mother did when she saw a mouse run across the kitchen floor, she went after it, your thoughts (like mine) will be different. Mice don't scare me a bit, because I don't believe there is anything to fear.

I'm interested in how and why people think the way they do. Admit it—you know someone right now whose thinking makes you wonder. I like to examine my own thinking and see where I can change it to make my life better.

Not surprisingly, being grateful is a fabulous way to change your thinking. It's so easy to dwell on what we don't have, or don't want, or don't like, but you can't have more than one thought in your head at one time.

So, if you look for something for which you can be thankful, that thought will displace whatever negative thoughts are swarming around in your brain. In fact, we can direct our thoughts whenever and however we want. Advice from the Bible again: "...keep your thoughts on whatever is right or deserves praise: things that are true, honourable, fair, pure, acceptable, or commendable."

Does this mean that we should all be Pollyanna types? Well, yes! Why not? The "Pollyanna Principle" is defined as the tendency for people to remember pleasant items more accurately than unpleasant ones. I'm all for that, aren't you?

A thing of beauty is a joy forever.
JOHN KEATS

So in the interest of spreading joy, here are some happy thoughts for you to think at Easter and for the rest of the month.

New babies are being born every day.
Spring always follows winter.
Fresh pineapple tastes wonderful.
Someone loves you.
You love someone.
Walking is free.
Aqua is a beautiful colour, especially in the sea.
The world is full of places to explore.
Reading a good book is a delightful escape.
There is no end of good books.
Libraries are free.
Kisses from toddlers are the best.
There are few things as sweet as a sleeping child.
Laughter is good for you.
Roses bloom and are always beautiful.
A glass of wine and a fire in the fireplace make a great pairing.
Having someone wash your hair feels like luxury.
Opportunities are everywhere.
Lambs on a green field are works of art.
Songbirds are like little spirits.
Giving blesses the giver as well as the receiver.
Jesus sacrificed his own life so we can be welcomed in heaven by a perfect, loving God. Believe it.

"Wow! My hair turned out great today," produces much happier thoughts than: "I have the worst hair ever!"

Remember, you get to choose the course of your life, and choosing what you think is where to start. We do not have to be prisoners of our thoughts. On the contrary! The Bible tells us that we can take every thought captive; to capture our thoughts and bring them into line. And it's not even difficult. You just have to pay attention.

There is much to be thankful for in our lives. Have a wonderful and blessed Easter!

Wendy

Beliefs are funny things. We often don't even realize that we have them until someone or something bumps up against them. (Remember your country's last election if you don't believe me.)

I love that changing a thought consistently will change a belief. As will simply making the decision to change the belief. If I look in the mirror and every day tell myself that I'm unattractive in some way, that's what I'll believe.

I can just as easily tell myself that I'm beautifully and wonderfully made, and this belief will produce a much happier feeling than the opposite. See how the thought precedes the feeling?

He is not here. He is Risen.
MARK 16:6

Dear Ones,

Well, it has been quite a week!

Last Tuesday I took a long-distance drive east from where I live in western British Columbia, to Calgary, Alberta, in the back seat of a pick-up truck accompanied by a nervous West Highland terrier named Jock.

In case you don't know, this is an all day drive: twelve hours, including short stops to eat, use bathrooms, and walk the dog (that is not mine, by the way).

The Rocky Mountains offer up a variety of weather conditions at this time of year. If it's spring at the west coast, there is no guarantee that it's not full-on winter at higher elevations.

On the east side of the continental divide we did run into snow—lots of it. Since I wasn't doing the driving, I decided it was a good time to take a nap.

After overnighting at my aunt's place north of Calgary, we pushed on to the farm in Saskatchewan. This was my third trip since January. Going places is always interesting.

While driving through the mountains delivers stunning, dramatic scenery, there is something about the prairies that easily rivals the attraction of peaks and forests—if you know how to look.

Lots of people have told me over the years that there is "nothing to see" on the prairies. I beg to differ.

While driving through the mountains, many of us expect to see some wild life: deer, elk, bears, mountain sheep, moose, maybe even a bear or two. I saw none of these in the mountains and hardly any birds. (They must have all been hiding.)

On the prairies I saw mule deer, antelope, owls, hawks, swans, geese, ducks, snipe and avocets (shore birds), muskrat, fox, and elk (they were farmed elk, but they count).

Meadowlarks sang from the tops of fence posts and despite the chilly weather, tiny flowers have already bloomed. The humble, furry crocus, also known as pasque flower, even made an appearance. They are the harbingers of every prairie spring.

When I was at my parents' house in February with my sister and sister-in-law, we got so much cleaning, sorting, and distributing done, including multiple trips to the thrift store and dumpster in town, that we felt like we had accomplished a lot.

The prairie farm has been in my family for over 100 years. Lots of living has taken place on those lands and a lot of memories are held within the walls of the house that my father built.

The humble crocus

Going back again last week felt like what remained to be done was still monumental. We had deliberately left mom's sewing room last time we were there as it was that room that most reflected her life.

This time we waded in to all the drawers, cupboards, two desks, and a tall filing cabinet. It still took us three days to clear it out.

There's something in you that pushes you in a certain direction, and you just have to go with it.

RUSSELL CAMPBELL

My mom was a passionate needle worker. She loved fibre arts, including embroidery, cross-stitch, and knitting, and was an expert seamstress. I'm so thankful that she made me learn how to do these things.

What was mind-boggling were the myriad of fabric scraps that she'd kept ("You never know when you might need that.") that served as reminders of dresses gone by.

A scrap of white sculptured velvet reminded me of the Christmas dress I designed and mom made for me when I was eleven or twelve.

I found a fragment of red sateen with tiny flowers from a dress she had made for me and I wore at my parents' twenty-fifth wedding anniversary. I was newly engaged at the time.

> *Enthusiasm is excitement with inspiration, motivation, and a pinch of creativity.*
> — BO BENNETT

(To give you some perspective, my wedding anniversary is in April and my husband and I celebrated over forty years of marriage. I was in Saskatchewan, mind you, while he was home in British Columbia, but still, it's something to celebrate.)

Speaking of passionate pursuits, I read something recently about concentrating on your passion being the secret ingredient to personal or business success. Do you think that's true?

> *Once something is a passion, the motivation is there.*
> — MICHAEL SCHUMACHER

I'm all for loving what you do, but it seems to me that we don't have to look far to "find" what we're passionate about. Try this exercise:

Get out a piece of paper and number it 1 - 25, down the left side. Then simply start writing a list of things you love.

What makes you happy just thinking about doing it or being there? Do you see any patterns? Does something jump out at you?

It's actually not that difficult to know what you love. You already know. It only becomes perplexing when you want to be passionate and make money from that passion at the same time.

Sometimes it works, and sometimes is doesn't. Still, we can always do things we love, or spend time in places that we love, if we're aware that it's always our choice.

> A woman knows by intuition, or instinct, what is best for herself.
> — MARILYN MONROE

On the other hand, sometimes it doesn't work out exactly right, but working out sort of right is a good alternative. For example, I love the beach. (If you follow me on Facebook, you already know that.) I would love to live at the beach, but do I? No. There are several reasons why not.

Canada doesn't have that many liveable beaches—most of British Columbia's coastline is more or less vertical. Moving means my husband has to be on board and because he works at a job where he'd like to stay for now, that's not so easy.

My solution is to visit beaches whenever I can. After all, they're always out there, so I know that the choice is always mine. I do things that remind me of what I love and want so I can keep my dreams alive and fresh.

I like to travel but big trips are not always available to me at the drop of a hat. So little trips to new destinations often suffice.

Dark chocolate finds its way onto my list of twenty-five things I love and is easy to indulge, thank goodness. The same goes for reading books. It's a seven-minute walk to my local library, so satisfying in my passion for reading is a piece of cake.

With that thought, I'll sign off for now.

Stay happy,

Hello, you Breath of Fresh Air,

I've been thinking a lot this week about spending time—how we spend it, and how quickly it can seemingly slip through our fingers.

Just think where you were or what you were doing a year ago. Doesn't it seem like it was just yesterday?

Life seems to zip by pretty fast. My little granddaughter will be three soon. Wow! That went fast. She'll soon be joined by a new sibling.

The fact is that life is made up of a series of moments, and when you pay attention to those moments, it gives you a different perspective than you get speeding through a daily to-do list.

On my blog this week, I wrote about how sometimes I want to do nothing. Doing nothing is a hard concept in modern life where being busy is glorified as something to be sought.

The older I get, the more disenchanted I've become with the idea that busyness as a goal is a good thing. As a follower of my blog pointed out, "When we've finished life, we won't look back with satisfaction on being too busy, but in watching hummingbirds and other lovely things. The things that will stand out will be our vacations and times with family and friends…"

© 2017 WENDY DEWAR HUGHES

I don't know about you, but I find the noise of everyday life, especially the input from media, to be an influence against which I have to guard my heart, if you will.

Besides the fact that noise prevents me from hearing myself, it also can sway me in ways that don't align with my true values.

Here is a simple example:

I got on the mailing list of a ladies' clothing store chain last year in exchange for a discount on something I purchased. No big deal.

Every day now, I get an email showing me pretty things I should buy because right now they're on sale, and they won't last, or the sale won't last. You know how it goes.

It's kind of fun looking at spring fashions, but it occurred to me that right now my priorities include paying off some debts, and saving for a vacation. As tempting as those floaty tops and cute shoes are, buying them now would work against my current values.

> *When your values are clear, making decisions becomes easier.*
> — ROY E. DISNEY

If I don't stop and think about it, I might just pop in to that store to have a look and come away with something I don't need, having spent the money I planned to use for something more important.

That's what I mean by noise.

When I sit by my window and quietly watch the clouds tumbling over the mountains, my heart is still. I can ask a question, and get an answer. If I'm always on the run, or have sounds assailing my ears, it's hard even to know what the questions are, much less hear an answer.

It's May already.

Where I live, the forsythia blossoms have come and gone. The rhododendrons are in bloom, and the trees are now almost in full leaf. At this latitude, spring can be slow in appearing, and this year it showed up well past fashionably late.

When I think about what I've had in mind for this year, it's shocking to realize that it's nearly half over already. My plans suffered a major jostling early in the year and the topsy-turvy results aren't over yet. This calls for adjustments to be made. But what?

I'm back to the same thought. If I can't see my way forward in the midst of rising anxiety and escalating demands because the noise is too loud, how will I navigate the remainder of the year and arrive at a destination that makes me happy?

There is a verse in the Bible that says: What good does it do you if you gain the whole world but lose your own soul?

My answer has to be, I'm working at the pace that works for me, which may not be the pace someone else believes I should set. The reason I can say that with peace is because I have spent time sitting by the window and contemplating the songbirds.

Does that seem like wasted time?

Does it make me look lazy in your eyes?

I hope not, but it doesn't matter if it does. You see, my opinion and God's opinion of me and how I live my life, are the most important ones. I care about the people with and for whom I work, but if I don't look after myself, I'll have nothing to give.

In order for me to have an ordered life, one free from unwanted anxiety (who ever wants anxiety, right?), it must include quiet, alone time. It must comprise time spent mulling over the demands of the day, sifting through them until the important nuggets rise to the top.

Great people have great values and great ethics.

JEFFREY GITOMER

If you imagine a sieve used to sort gravel or grain, the motion of the hands causes the tiny, dusty particles to fall away, leaving the larger, more important pieces. My contemplation works something like that.

As the silence of the morning settles in the room, I sift through the demands before me, allowing the less important to drop away so that the vital and the valuable are left. Without the chaff, I can clearly see the fragments that remain; the ones that count.

> I think sometimes the best training is to rest.
> CHRISTIANO RONALDO

Writing this monthly letter turns up among those activities that count. My commitment to inspiring my readers to live true to yourself and your values is high on my list. Throughout my life, people have come alongside me and encouraged me when I've needed it, no matter what I was doing.

With this letter, my goal is to encourage you in following the pursuits that you love. Seek the beauty, the peaceful, and the joyous. They are found through quiet attention and calm reflection.

Rest easy,
Wendy

Hello Gorgeous!

After much waiting and wondering, it looks like summer (or at least late spring) has decided to make an appearance. A robin has a nest in the forsythia tree in my front yard and keeps sneaking in and out of the foliage to her little hide-out.

One of the most difficult things I've had to do for the past several months is to remain upbeat for others while feeling drained myself. You've probably experienced something similar at one time or other. It happens when in the face of life's discouragements, you still have to go on.

That can mean going on at work like there's nothing else happening, but you're dealing with a serious health issue. Or, showing up in other public situations as though everything is normal when something in your personal life is causing anguish or emotional pain, or is just plain falling apart.

We put on a brave face to the world because we believe that no one wants to know about our difficulties. And sometimes, we'd be right. Sometimes others don't want to know.

That's why we have to be selective about what we tell to whom. It's not that we even want advice. What we want is to be real and to have someone else acknowledge our troubles. The telling itself is healing. Keeping things bottled up inside often means that they swirl around and around in our own minds and find no resolution.

I don't mean to get all heavy on you, but I know that what I've experienced over the past few months is not peculiar to me. We can't get through life completely unscathed. It simply doesn't work like that.

Writing out what's on your mind or heart can really help to process whatever is going on. If you journal, you'll know what I mean. However, sometimes you want to know that someone "hears" you. If you ever feel like need that, why not write it in a letter? You can even write to me. I'm a good listener, and everything is always confidential. I'm the soul of discretion.

On a lighter note, my husband and I managed to get away for the week last week for a long overdue break. Since we live close to the US border and love to visit "foreign" countries, we headed south. We had a wonderful, relaxing time. The weather wasn't grand but we had some sunny days. It's so fantastic for me to walk along a beach, regardless of the weather, and hear the waves crashing. At Ocean Shores, WA, the beach is long and wide and when those waves crash, they slide so far onto the flat beach that you can walk and walk in an inch of water.

Having tried that, though, once a big wave came in and hit the bottom of my rolled up jeans before I could scamper inland. Never mind that the water is like ice in the Pacific, especially this time of year. Once your bare feet have grown accustomed to the cold (also known as numb) it's still fun to try to outrun the waves as they come ashore.

A day by the water is good for the soul.

I've been home since last weekend but getting back into the groove of working has been a challenge. A bunch of stuff had to be dealt with right away, and at the same time several work projects clamour for my attention.

Everthing requires a sole focus, something that's so difficult to achieve amidst multiple demands. I know it's not humanly possible to do everything at once. Yet concentrating on one thing at a time is a skill that's still a bit out of reach for me.

I dislike the feeling of being behind on my work or obligations, which is why I've chosen the concept of simplifying and paying attention as my goals this year.

It's really a matter of knowing the difference between the urgent and the important. And knowing your values and goals. Such a big subject.

People often ask me how I get so much done. I usually think, "Ack! I'm nowhere near done!"

I would like to say I have a system for looking after everything. I really would like to say that—and have one. Just before leaving on vacation, all the boxes of things from my mom's house arrived, along with the dining room suite that I have inherited. Needless to say, I didn't get much of that dealt with before going away, so naturally it was all waiting for me when I came back in the door. All week, I've been stepping over boxes and their contents as I've sorted through them.

Some of what came to my house has to be separated out and taken to my two daughters. Opening the boxes again sometimes makes me sad, and other times makes me shake my head. "Why did I say I'd take these?" I ask, holding a pair of turquoise plastic earrings from the 1960s. Or the vase that goes with nothing in my house and I have no place to store.

Usually, the closest I come to using a system during overwhelm is to pay attention to the most urgent thing first. I remember many years ago reading an article called, The Tyranny of the Urgent.

Yes, urgency can certainly be a tyrant, and it can keep you from doing the important. It's hard to remember when you're up to your bottom in alligators that your job is to drain the swamp.

Often when I feel I need a vacation the most is when the opportunity is simply not available. Other times, when it feels like the alligators are nipping at my pant legs is when my husband announces that he's booked time off from his job and we're taking a break. "Noooo," I wail. "Yes," he insists. "You need it." Such a smart man.

Getting back to vacations...we were talking about that, weren't we? Anyway, it seems to me that what we humans like best is to play.

We all like to play, and most of us feel like we don't have enough play in our lives. One way around this and also dealing with the "making a living" issue, is to choose work that feels like play.

I realize that not everyone needs this, nor does everyone manage to make it happen, but if you can spend as much time as possible doing things you love, or finding something to love in what you do, you'll be happier.

So since it's the weekend when this is going out, be sure to do something that feels like play to you. It can be as simple as reading a book, or as "big" as taking up a new sport or craft. Keep in mind that the goal is to have fun.

Stay happy!

Wendy

I think that success is having fun.
BRUNO MARS

Well hello,

When I was a young mother, department stores would have special sales on baby things, which was the time to stock up on togs for little ones. One store called theirs "Baby Week".

Well, it's baby week here soon as my daughter is about to pop out her second wee one, literally any day now. Aside from the obvious thrill of another grandchild, this grandma is being called upon to swoop into action to go stay with my almost-three-year-old granddaughter while her mama and daddy bring the new one into the family.

That means dropping everything and hitting the road for their house. It's not usual for the grandmother to have to have her suitcase packed for the impending birth, but I'm up for it. I haven't packed yet, but that won't take but a few minutes (she says, totally kidding herself.)

With new baby on the family brain, someone's dolly needs diapers. So I had to dig my sewing machine out from the piles of stuff that I'm still trying to sort through from my mom's sewing room, then dust it off and get to work. Here is the result so far. Pretty cute, right?

Next week is also a birthday week in our family. My other daughter is hitting a milestone birthday. I've forbidden her from sharing her actual age as it's starting reflect on mine. She has planned an art gallery scavenger hunt to celebrate. Such a creative idea! I can't wait to see how that turns out.

I read on Facebook today that somewhere, Texas, I think, is talking about heat warnings. All I can say is, we could use a bit of that. Heavy cloud and rain makes me think this is more like "Junuary" than June. Some folks like it cool, but as you've probably realized by now, I'm a summer girl.

Where I live, we're surrounded by mountains but I live on the valley floor. About a ten minute drive away is a huge lake and up in among the mountains are smaller lakes. With summer just about here in earnest (one keeps hoping) it's time to dust the spiders out of the canoe, and break out the flip-flops.

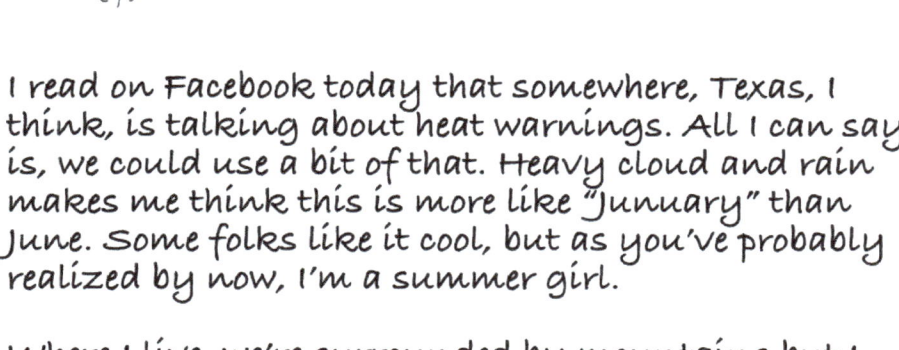

I'm not really the outdoorsy type, but several years ago I gave my husband a canoe for his birthday, and well, a guy doesn't want to go canoeing alone, so guess who gets to paddle along? Truth be told, we're fair weather canoeists, and as often as I can get away with it, I lounge and let him paddle. It's his canoe, after all, right?

I have to admit that a quiet paddle around a small mountain lake is pretty good therapy for clearing the head. It's not the only strategy I use, since most of the year the lake is inaccessible. A walk around the neighbourhood, or a half hour in the garden are also effective.

I've come to value quiet and a slow pace more these days. I have always been a wanderer, even when I was young. I remember days where I grew up, wandering around the farm, poking into the usual haunts alone as the prairie wind lifted my hair and the sun browned my face. Open spaces are good for the soul.

I still like walking as a remedy for melancholy or fretfulness. Now, I choose the streets in my village where few people walk so I can be alone with my thoughts. From my house, it takes me about five minutes to get to the community gardens.

There is rarely anyone there, or if so, it's usually only one or two folks tending garden patches. The gardens are at the end of a small road so there is no other traffic and no one walks down that street. Walking around the garden plots, I can watch the progression of the seasons.

I love gardens, but right now I don't want to invest the time they require for upkeep. It is a matter of priorities, since there are only so many hours in the day, and I know my own energy level—it's not high and never has been.

Serious gardening has to wait.

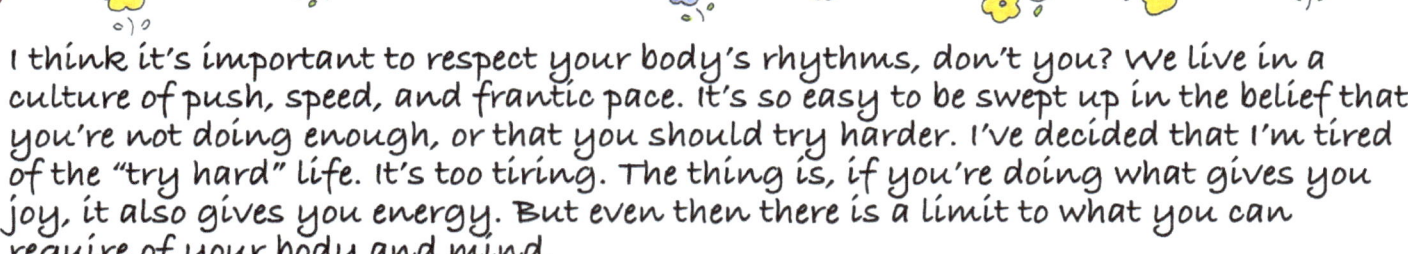

I think it's important to respect your body's rhythms, don't you? We live in a culture of push, speed, and frantic pace. It's so easy to be swept up in the belief that you're not doing enough, or that you should try harder. I've decided that I'm tired of the "try hard" life. It's too tiring. The thing is, if you're doing what gives you joy, it also gives you energy. But even then there is a limit to what you can require of your body and mind.

Without proper rest, relaxation, and "do nothing" time, we'll wear out. I want to last a long time because I have a long list of things I want to do and I don't want to try to do them all at once. It's important that I don't exhaust myself in the process.

As I was creating this letter, the power went out. Ack! So much of what we do relies on electricity. I scanned a mental list of things to do since my computer wasn't available and had to discard everything that required power.

Fortunately, there is always reading, and it can be done by candlelight. At this latitude, nearing the longest days of the year, it stays light until after 10:00 PM. Lucky for me, the electricity came back on after a couple of hours.

Speaking of babies, though it's still in its infancy, I've added a shop to my website at

www.summerbaystudio.com

New things are appearing regularly. Head over there and take a look and keep checking for new products as they come on board.

If you think of things you'd like to see in my shop, please let me know and I'll try to make them available.

Have a happy week, or weekend. Next time I write, I'll be able to brag on my new grandbaby.

Sweetness,

Dear lovelies,

After a long wait, and then some, (on the part of my daughter) my little grandson arrived on a Friday afternoon in June. This wee boy weighed in at 10 lbs, 7 oz, and is my first (maybe only) grandson. What a sweet gift! Here he is only a few hours old.

With two daughters, we've had a girly family so I'm sure it will be a whole new fun adventure having a boy. His grandpa is pretty excited about that and can't wait to see him.

Mom and baby are thriving—some sleepless nights notwithstanding.

To everything there is a season...
Ecclesiastes 3:1

Everything is in bloom where I live and it is such a joy to see all the colours of summer on display. Spring time seemed to slide by in a string of days (many of them grey) so when summer bursts into bloom, I'm happy.

All these photos are from my own flowers. The hanging basket is filled with calibrachoa, a name that I only just learned. The shasta daisies, above, are perennials so only bloom once. This one attracted a busy bee.

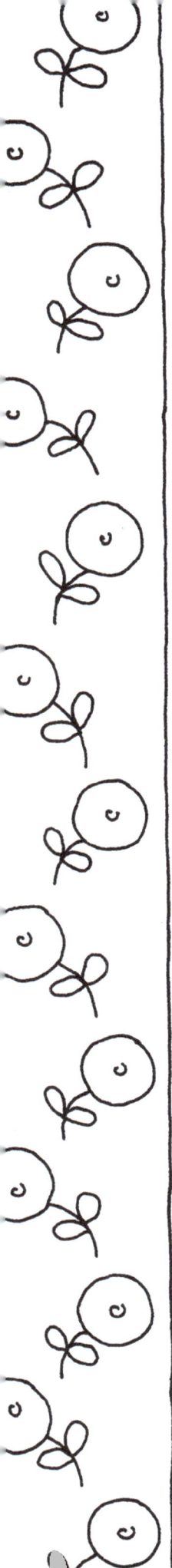

July 1st is Canada Day which is Canada's national holiday. Lots of celebrations are going on all over the country. Pancake breakfasts, stage presentations, parades, and amusements abound. It is a statutory holiday so most employees get the day off.

I picked up bedding plants for my flowerbeds a few days ago—late, I know, but it has been a busy, and cold, spring. At this late date, it's not surprising that selection is limited, but it worked in my favour anyway. I found red and white petunias to match Canada's flag, just in time for the Canada Day celebrations. Pretty, aren't' they?

It doesn't take a lot to make things better. Little changes can make a difference. The patch of bare dirt in my flower bed, with very little cost and effort becomes a mass of blossoms. My containers also suddenly-overflow with colour.

Listen to the colour of your dreams.
THE BEATLES

Have you ever embarked on something new and been stopped in your tracks because the whole thing seemed suddenly too big and daunting? Ugh! That's when procrastination usually shows up. You want to do whatever it is but can't get started.

I know we've all been there. I sure have. But there is a solution that I've found works really well for me. Read on...

The problem is seeing the whole picture at once. When you view the entire scope of a project, whether it's writing a book, painting a room, or shopping for shoes, it can seem enormous. However, if you break it down into smaller pieces, and simply focus on each step at a time, it becomes manageable. Before you know it, you'll have finished.

For example, when all the boxes and bags of things that I inherited from my parents arrived at the door, my entire small house was in shambles. Where would I put everything? Every space was already stuffed. Rather than despairing over the enormity of the job, I decided to take it a little bit at a time and not to mind having to step around things until places were found. It has taken nearly two months and there is still a bag or two that I need to deal with, but the job is getting done without causing myself a lot of unnecessary stress.

From small beginnings come great things.

PROVERB

Colour the sidebars

Now that summer is officially here—according to the calendar—it's time to think about summer projects and decorating. I like to change out the colours in my living room with pretty cloths or mats on the tables, and accessories that reflect the season.

I collect flamingos, and I love anything beachy, so pinks and aqua/turquoise move in as the spring colours get put away. When I cut flowers and bring them inside, I also like to accessorize around them in coordinating colours to show them off as a focal point.

As I mentioned, I don't have a large house and storage space is at a premium, so I lean toward small touches when it comes to setting a seasonal mood.

We've been led to believe that bigger is always better, but that can result in always feeling vaguely dissatisfied with what we have. There will always be others who have more material possessions, or seem to be living a more "shining" life. By comparing ourselves to those folks who have more, we see ourselves as lacking, or being in a state of lack. Not a comfortable place to be at all—but it's an emotion.

Another choice is to appreciate what we do have. Enough food for today, a cozy bed in which to sleep, people who love us, and interesting things to do are all precious things that make up a valuable life.

Love and long-distance hugs for now,

(I picked this little guy up last weekend at an art store.)

The Joys of July

It's no secret to those who know me that I love summer. In fact, July is my favourite month, followed closely by August, and June.

There is plenty to do in July that you can't or won't want to do in other months. This letter is about fun things to try this month to make your entire summer more enjoyable, relaxing, and memorable.

Here goes!

1. Wear sandals. Put away your closed-toe shoes for the season and get out your flip flops. Go barefoot whenever you can. It makes your feet stronger.

2. Treat yourself to a pedicure. Or, DIY after your bath or shower. Pick a pretty nail polish colour that reminds you of hibiscus flowers or tropical seas.

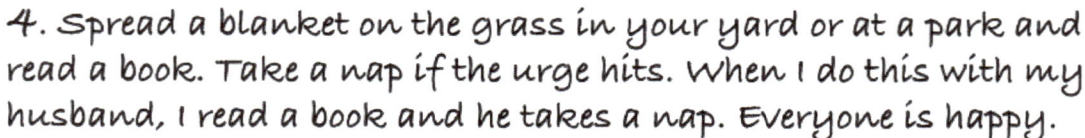

3. Go swimming. Take a dip in the ocean, the lake, or the local pool. Just so you know, no one cares what you look like in your swim suit. Take your body to the beach and voilà! You have a beach body.

4. Spread a blanket on the grass in your yard or at a park and read a book. Take a nap if the urge hits. When I do this with my husband, I read a book and he takes a nap. Everyone is happy.

5. Ride your bicycle. If you need a destination or focus, try counting something such as tree species, or bird sightings. Or, ride to the nearest (or farthest) ice cream shop and order a rocky road cone.

6. Go to a festival. Country fairs, arts and music festivals, and special events happen all summer long. When was the last time you went to a rodeo, a car show, or an outdoor theatre production? Order a ticket today.

7. Drink lemon iced tea. So refreshing!

8. Make this refreshing Melon Granita recipe.

6 cups seedless melon chunks or balls
1 Tbsp lemon juice
1 Tbsp lime juice
½ cup ginger ale

1. PUREE the melon, lemon juice, and lime juice in a blender. Slowly pour into the ginger ale and mix.

2. POUR into an 8" x 8" metal pan (not nonstick). Cover with plastic wrap and freeze for one hour.

3. STIR with a fork, breaking up the chunks. Cover and return to the freezer. Stir every 30 minutes for 2½ hours or until the mixture is evenly icy and granular. Enjoy with a straw or spoon.

Every summer has its own story.

9. Go boating. Rent a canoe or a kayak (if you don't already have one) and head out onto the water. Don't forget to wear your life jacket.

10. Take a day trip. Make your plan the night before and include some scenic stops or pretty shops. Eat at a local restaurant that isn't a national chain.

11. Pick a theme for the month. It can be anything, from bird spotting, to wearing more colour, to exploring your local library. Pick something you've always wanted to do and give it a try for the rest of the month.

12. Pack a picnic and eat outside. Use throw-away dishes and cutlery for easy clean-up and keep the menu simple. Cold cuts, crusty buns, veggies and dip, pickles, followed by fruit for dessert make for quick and simple picnic fare.

13. Get a sketchbook and draw your surroundings. All you need is a pencil, a sharpener, and a rubber eraser (they don't tear the paper). Yes, it is perfectly permissable to erase lines and re-draw. That's how you learn.

Summer.
Hair gets lighter.
Skin gets darker.
Water gets warmer.
Drinks get colder.
Music gets louder.
Nights get longer.
Life gets better.

14. Star gaze. On a clear night, go far away from city lights, lie on your back in the grass and look up at the stars. The lower the humidity, the clearer the sky will be, so watch the weather forecast for a good night then discover the Milky Way again.

15. Get up early and go for a sunrise walk. Before the heat of the day is intense, take a walk when all is still quiet and cool.

16. Visit the zoo. If you have children in your life, take them with you. Their joy and excitement add to the fun for everyone. Pick out your favourite animal.

17. Grill Peaches

4 medium peaches, halved and pits removed
4 coconut macaroons
¼ cup caramel or chocolate topping

1. HEAT grill to medium and coat the rack with cooking spray.

2. PLACE peaches cut side down on grill rack and grill until lightly browned and tender, about 10 minutes, turning once. Remove and arrange 2 halves on each of four dessert plates.

3. CRUMBLE macaroons into cavities and over tops.

4. DRIZZLE topping evenly over all. Delicious!

18. Go to a drive-in movie theatre. Take your pillow, eat popcorn, and snuggle with your sweetie. Or take the kids and put a blanket on the hood of the car for them.

The tans will fade but the summer memories will last forever.

19. Play mini-golf. Visit a local mini-golf or pitch and putt course and play a round. Go with friends and host a contest with prizes for the best scores, worst shots, or craziest golf hat.

20. Pick berries or tree fruit in the field or roadside. Strawberry time may be just about over, but cherries and peaches are in season, and blackberries are free along the roadsides if they grow where you live.

21. Start a collection. Seashells, pine cones, or kitchy kitchen utensils all make fun things to collect. Think about the things that frequently catch your eye when you're out and about, or while watching TV. For example, I always notice antique inkwells so I have started collecting a few. I also collect flamingo-themed objects.

22. Paint by numbers, or get a colouring book and colour your days. (My colouring books, Sketches from the South of France, and Le Petit Paris are both available from Amazon.)

Sunshine is my favourite accessory.

23. Spend time in the garden, or grow some flowers and vegetables in containers if you have only a small space. Even herbs on your window-sill count as gardening.

24. Plan a trip. If you can't get away this summer, start planning for your next vacation or getaway. Anticipation is part of the fun. Don't be afraid to daydream about the trip of your dreams. That's where they all start, after all.

25. Read a summer romance. I have written several short romantic fiction novellas that perhaps you will enjoy. They are vailable on Amazon, Kindle, iBooks, Barnes and Noble and more. Simply go to my website at www.wendydewarhughes.com and click on My Books.

Whatever makes summer exciting and fun, be sure to do lots of it. Summer is only here for a short time.

Have a great July! *Wendy*

Hello dear!

I've discovered an author whose writing I particularly like. Actually, it's not just the writing, which we all know is not the "everything" of a book; it's also the stories.

Lately, I've had the itch to travel and since I'm not able to until later this year, I like to read books that take place in locations where I want to go. I've been feeling a bit "homesick" for France, where I lived for a while several years ago.

I've also had a yen to go to the UK, Cornwall and Scotland in particular. I came across the Doc Martin television series at the local library recently and love nothing better than to watch an entire series, one episode after another. The Doc Martin series takes place in, you guessed it, a village in Cornwall. Of course, it makes me want to go see the area.

The novels I've been reading by various authors have taken place in Paris, and in Scotland. I have travelled to both of those destinations but it was many years ago. In fact, sometimes it all seems like a long ago dream.

But here's the thing. We all know that what you think about most tends to show up in your life, whether it's trouble on your job, or the coat in a store window that caught your eye. Our minds will drift to whatever we decide to think about, consciously or unconsciously.

This tells me that if I want something to grow larger in my life, then thinking about it will help me to focus on achieving it or bringing it into being. We tend to gravitate toward what we think about most.

A couple of months ago, I did a search on the library site for the word "summer". We had a prolonged cold winter and spring where I live and it seemed like summer would never start. But I wanted to experience it right then so I requested several novels about summer. If I can't yet go outside without a coat, I can enjoy summer vicariously through someone else's experience—even fictional—can't I?

Now, I knew that summer is going to come eventually, and when it did, well, it has been fabulous (except for all the forest fires and resulting smoke). But there are many things that won't come automatically just because we wish they would.

If I'm going to visit Paris, I need to take the thought of going there and allow it space to grow. One way to do that is to keep reminders in front of your eyes, hence the books that take place there.

I call it, feeding the dream.

First you decide what you want, then you begin to pay attention to it, dwell on it, imagine yourself already having achieved it, and love the thought of enjoying it. This is your starting place. After that comes a plan.

I believe so strongly in this method of getting what you wish for that I created a whole program around it. It's called The Wish Plan (www.thewishplan.com) and is so easy to do once you know how.

I don't really believe in magic, but I do believe in miracles. I also believe in simply getting off your chair and going after what you want.

Who can't think of dozens of reasons not to do something? Ask your friends or family members if you want to find out why you shouldn't do whatever you'd like. They'll have plenty of reasons, probably some you haven't even thought of yet.

Years ago, when I decided I really, really, really wanted to live in France for a while, the first people I told were my children. They just believed that if mom said it, it would be so. Having that kind of validation felt pretty sweet.

Dreams are like babies. They must be fed if they are to grow.

As time went on and it became clear to the adults in my life that I was pretty serious about doing this crazy thing, all their reasons not to do it came pouring out.

How could I uproot my family like that?
What about the house we owned?
Was I really leaving my job?
How would we support ourselves?
What about the kids' schooling?

Then there were the more personal ones:

How can you be so selfish?
How could you do that to your children?
Are you crazy?
Why on earth would you want to leave here?

I could go on, but you probably get the picture. (My point isn't that you should want what I want, or want to see the world. You must honour your own life. Perhaps all you want to do is change your hair colour, or learn to paint.)

Opposition will come as soon as you make a decision. Oftentimes, it's just that nasty little voice in your head that tells you not to be silly, or makes you feel vaguely guilty.

Do it anyway.

Practically up until we were stepping on the plane to make our move to Europe, people were still offering their negative opinions about what we had decided to do.

We did it anyway. Those opinions made no difference to the wonderful time we had living in the South of France.

Once we were no longer in view, all those people with all their well-meaning advice and opinions, which by the way, were based on their own fears and inadequacies, just melted away.

What we derived from the experience of following my big dream of living in France has been lifelong for my immediate family and for me. Going after the big dream changed us all, in so many positive ways. We could have not done it but there was a moment when I said to my husband, "I don't want to get to be sixty-five years old and wish that we had gone." That was motivation enough—the fear of regret.

No matter what's going on in your life, discouragement will happen. At times like these, it's important to remind yourself that this is your one life, and you have the opportunity now to make it look like you want it to, regardless of your age or complications. We all deserve to have happiness, and no one else can tell you what that looks like for you.

This pep talk is for me as much as anyone reading this letter. Sometimes I feel overwhelmed, inadequate, not up to the challenge, and just plain tired. But I also know that dreams can come true.

If I have made mine come true once, I can do it again. And so can you.

Love,
Wendy

P.S. Never stop dreaming your beautiful dreams.

Dear Gentle Reader,

Here we are already at the end of July (my favourite month), and it seems like summer has only just begun. I can almost feel my heels skidding as the calendar marches toward fall.

This has been an eventful year at my house—and not always in a good way. It has become a time of counting up the losses (eight friends and family passed away so far this year), and keeping a lookout for positives in all of this.

Family is the most important aspect of our lives and I've been thinking a lot about that recently. Both my parents are now gone, which is still hard to comprehend. Today my sister, who has lived within a ten-minute drive from my house for over twenty years, is leaving to move across the country to Quebec.

Babies napping in the shade. Finley has trouble keeping his eyes open on such a lazy day.

> You don't choose your family. They are God's gift to you, as you are to them.
> — DESMOND TUTU

> Change your thoughts and you change your world.
> — NORMAL VINCENT PEALE

My granddaughter, Zoë (3), right, getting to know her second cousin, Maya, (2).

We were talking yesterday about how this turn of events could have happened, since two years ago, our futures looked entirely different. (Goes to show how little we know about what is ahead for each of us.)

But one thing happens that angles your course direction a little, and then another event or experience comes along. A decision is made based on the information at hand, but something else tweaks that decision so the outcome is different. Before you know it you're on an entirely different path.

On the bright side, my little grandson, Finley, was born in June, evidently completing our expected roster of grandchildren to a total of two. We're thrilled and will take all we can get but one daughter isn't having children, and the other says she's done. So two sweeties it is. The family grows and love encompasses everyone.

Now my parents' generation is doing the unthinkable yet inevitable and dying off. Time rolls along and my generation take its place as the "grands". Extended family becomes more important, and new in-laws fill in gaps in the numbers.

Love is like elastic. It stretches to fit everyone.

Today is my husband's birthday so on the weekend we had a party. Since the weather has been so fabulously summer, we had an outdoor barbecue picnic, complete with babies, toddlers, and grandmas. How delightful it is to watch a newborn sleep on a blanket spread out on the grass, not a care in the world.

Burgers, salad, lemonade, ice cream, and cake made the perfect—and simple—menu for the day. It was a combination farewell for my sister and her husband, hello/goodbye to my niece and her husband and children, who live in Quebec, and birthday party for my husband. Sort of a "one party fits all".

What is this life if, full of care, We have no time to stand and stare. No time to stand beneath the boughs And stare as long as sheep or cows. No time to see, when woods we pass, Where squirrels hide their nuts in grass. No time to see, in broad daylight, Streams full of stars, like skies at night.

WM. HENRY DAVIES

Since cleaning out my parents' home on the farm over the months from February to April, I've taken a jaundiced view at all the "extra" stuff in my own house. I want to lighten my load because having too much stuff to deal with actually steals energy that can be put to good use doing things that either move you in the direction of your fondest dreams, or give you a more peaceful life.

I listened to a TED talk yesterday about overwhelm, and how it is common to so many people these days. We have full-time work, family demands, volunteer commitments, have church and club obligations, personal needs, meals to cook and clean up after, and homes to clean and maintain. It kind of leaves you breathless just thinking about it all.

The summer clearance sales are now on—one of my favourite things! But I'm not shopping because my closet needs reduction, not addition. I love summer clothes, but because I work alone at home most of the time, my wardrobe needs are few. Sometimes I don't even have a chance to wear my clothes from last year.

And I hesitate even to mention the topic of shoes. I gave away two bags of them a few weeks ago, finally admitting that having them sit in my closet for another year would not enhance my life.

The interesting thing about de-cluttering your surroundings is that it has the effect of de-cluttering your mind, too. Not having to deal with so many details frees up space to think about what's really important.

Case in point: if someone close to you suddenly needs you, whether because there has been an accident, a fire, an illness, a death, or something else, priorities suddenly become clear. The little things that tangle up our lives and sap the joy out of our days instantly become irrelevant and unnecessary.

Many years ago, a death in my family prompted me to drop everything and fly to Europe for a month. On the flight home I had plenty of time to examine my life and recognize what really mattered to me. I was a volunteer on committees at my children's schools, jobs I felt compelled to do but took little joy in.

Almost as soon as I got off that airplane, I resigned from those committees. I like to think that my departure made room for someone to step in who genuinely derived joy from the work, but even if that weren't the case, I needed to redeem that time for my own life and work.

I realize I'm wandering a bit this time, but that's what letter writing is all about, isn't it? Given the blows that I've experienced this year so far, I've stepped back to assess again what I'm doing with my days, that ultimately make up my life. I'm not in my twenties anymore, with the future spreading out before me like a long road stretching into the hazy distance.

Lately, I've missed having time to make more art. I need that to be a more regular part of my life. Why? It was what I was born to do.

I've never been one to sit and wish things could be different but not do anything to make them change. Instead, I ask myself what I want my life to look like now, and what needs to happen to make that vision a reality.

So here's what's going on so far. My art cabinet is crammed with watercolours that I've created over the years. I have lots of art that that was very popular when I had my wholesale gift stationery business. And I paint new watercolours regularly. Phrases and sayings that appeared on my work in the past, still make people smile, or laugh, and will appear again.

Now that the Internet has made worldwide distribution and print-on-demand possible without needing to own your own warehouse, my designs are going on multiple products so they'll be available from anywhere with a few clicks of your mouse.

> If you ask me what I came to do in this world, I, an artist, will answer you: I am here to live out loud.
> — EMILE ZOLA

I devote as much time as I can to creating new designs for multiple products online. I love doing this; it has always been a dream and passion of mine to create and sell my watercolour designs on fun and useful products, as well as in books and paper products.

I will let you know more about the new developments in my next letter, but for now, be sure to check the shop on my website at www.wendydewarhughes.com.

Until next time, enjoy your summer!

hello september!

Wow! Can you believe that August has already gone! I always hope that it will pass slowly but it never does.

Have you ever looked at a decorating magazine or book, then looked around your house and suddenly thought about all the things you'd like to change or update? It's almost like seeing it for the first time.

The cute curtains in the magazine make yours look blah and tired. The sagging armchair where your husband falls asleep watching the evening news now looks like something you found in a back alley.

wait, what? that can't be right...

Even the paint looks somehow 1970s even though it has only been on the walls for what? Seven years? Or, maybe ten. Wait, you re-painted when your youngest went off to university, which was in 1993. That can't be right...

I recently watched a series of Netflix shows about people shopping for new homes with a view. After each one, I wanted to live near a vineyard, get a float house in the harbour, move to a tall Victorian overlooking a beach, or snuggle into an adobe ranch house with desert views and a massive stone fireplace.

We don't usually want to admit it, but what we are exposed to changes how we think. Like magpies picking up shiny objects, we all have our heads turned by what catches our attention.

this can act as a warning, or it can be extremely good news. or both. here's why:

If I have something in my life that is not making me happy, it would be a good idea for me to ask myself what I'm paying attention to. For example, there is a call-in discussion program on the radio here in Canada that I turn on when I'm making my lunch.

The topics generally reflect what's going on in the news media, and are often about what the government or some organization is doing. People phone in and share their opinions on the topic.

While I am often not interested in the subject of discussion, I have to admit to being irritated by some of the comments of the call-in listeners, so much so that I find myself talking back to them while I savagely slice my cold chicken breast into shreds.

what is happening? more importantly, do i want to feel like this?

Do I want to know more about why a city in which I don't live should or shouldn't raise bus fares?

When I become aware of how the input is affecting me internally, rather than being caught up in the external that is going on, my perspective changes. I turn off the radio, get out a magazine about travelling down a scenic road, and voilà! My day instantly changes.

here's a look at the positive side:

When I decided I wanted to live in France some years ago (actually, it didn't feel like I decided so much as God decided for me), I turned my attention in that direction.

Once I could see my goal, I added to it with plans and possibilities. It took a while to come to pass, but my family and I did indeed go to France to live.

At this time in my life I want to travel more, do more fun things, and meet new people. Knowing that, I can turn my attention to including more of those needs. At the same time, I will turn my attention away from what I don't want.

When my children were young, we used to go on family vacations in a 1973 Volkswagon camper van. We loved that van because it represented freedom and holidays to us, even though the springs in the front seats poked into our backs and the mattress was like sleeping on the living room floor.

oh, but the adventures we had.

We have all travelled a lot since those days, and still do. It gets in your blood and makes your feet itchy to go new places, see new vistas, and experience new things.

This year, with its many ups, downs, and sideways blows, has reminded me that life here on good old earth doesn't last forever. If I want to do something, I had better get with it. In the same way I decided to go to France because I didn't want to get to my sixties or seventies and wish I had, I've decided I want to create more art—for the fun of it. (I have another novel in mind too, but more about that later.)

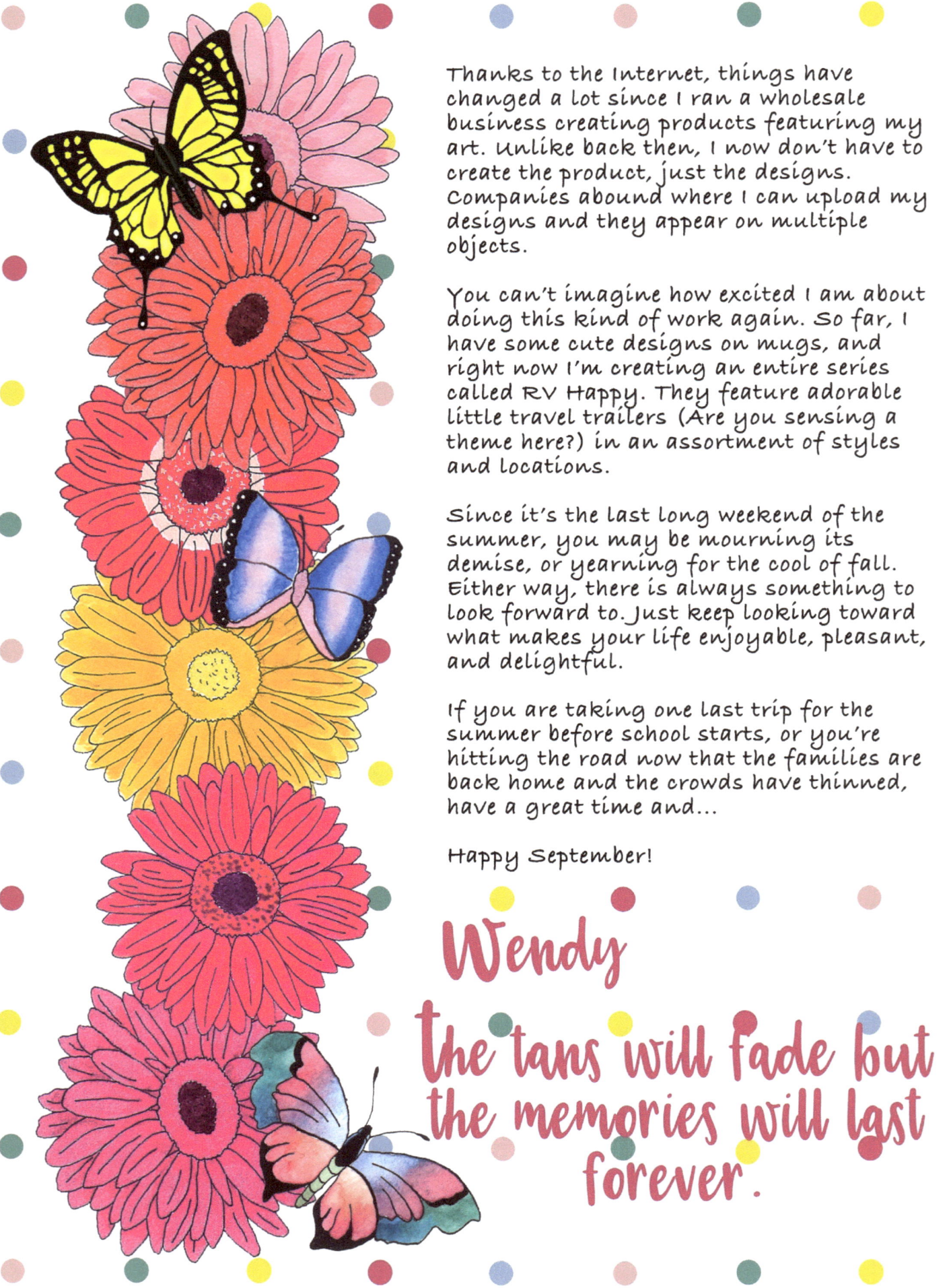

Thanks to the Internet, things have changed a lot since I ran a wholesale business creating products featuring my art. Unlike back then, I now don't have to create the product, just the designs. Companies abound where I can upload my designs and they appear on multiple objects.

You can't imagine how excited I am about doing this kind of work again. So far, I have some cute designs on mugs, and right now I'm creating an entire series called RV Happy. They feature adorable little travel trailers (Are you sensing a theme here?) in an assortment of styles and locations.

Since it's the last long weekend of the summer, you may be mourning its demise, or yearning for the cool of fall. Either way, there is always something to look forward to. Just keep looking toward what makes your life enjoyable, pleasant, and delightful.

If you are taking one last trip for the summer before school starts, or you're hitting the road now that the families are back home and the crowds have thinned, have a great time and...

Happy September!

Wendy

the tans will fade but the memories will last forever.

Hello, my dears!

I had every intention of writing last week but came home with a nasty cold that knocked me off my feet. Then, I was scheduled to attend a four day conference on the weekend while still sniffling. That's life, isn't it?

Now that I'm feeling a little better, I am so excited to take you on my retrospective tour of Quebec and slightly beyond. I took lots of photos so I can tell you all about my trip. I like armchair travel nearly as much as the real thing—but not quite.

It began in the (very) wee hours of September 11th. Our clocks were set to 2:30 AM (gak!) as our flight was scheduled to depart at 6:00 AM. As it is an hour's drive from my house to the airport, and you never know if there will be some slowdown on the highway, we always want to leave a little wiggle room. Hence our short night, and early morning.

My sister had plans for us to do lots of fun things so we didn't hesitate to get started. One of our day trips took us to the village of Knowlton, which is where author Louise Penny lives and is also the model for her fictitious village of Three Pines.

Hydrangeas were everywhere, turning such beautiful colours in late summer.

The hotel and bistro in Knowlton, (right) immortalized in many of Louise Penny's novels.

Nearby is also Lac Brome, which is famous for Brome ducks.

Antique shops are everywhere and this was a particularly interesting one in Knowlton. My sister bought a lovely old wooden chair.

Where my sister and brother-in-law moved is right near the US border, southwest of Montreal. One day, they had an appointment to get Quebec drivers' licenses, which evidently is kind of a big deal there. The government office was in a town about halfway to Montreal, so we decided it would be a good day to visit the old town of Montreal, which was first settled in the 1600s.

However, on the way we were detoured due to road construction and missed our exit. This took us right past Atwater Market, a huge farmers' market. Just look at this beautiful produce!

Fruits and vegetables abound everywhere you look. Stalls for cheeses, meats, flowers, and lavender stretch almost as far as you can see. It's almost like a market in Europe, except that the prices are listed in Canadian dollars.

The streets in Montreal resemble streets in cities and towns in France. See, there is even a French flag hanging up above the market umbrellas. Those cheeky Quebecers!

The weather was so warm.

Old Montreal

Montreal is an old city with plenty of fascinating history. It was founded on May 17th, 1642.

The square in front of the cathedral (left). The Notre Dame Basilica (right).

We arrived about five minutes before closing at the massive cathedral so we weren't able to go inside. I had been there once, several years ago, and can tell you, it is spectacular.

Instead we wandered through the old part of the city, checked out a few shops, listened to street musicians, and people-watched.

The old architecture is fascinating and beautiful. So elegant and decorative — and all in stone.

We had a lovely dinner in a small restaurant.

I also found this delicious stationery store nearby. Paper, inks, pens, cards — oh my!

Antiques Market! Ooh la la!

Hot, sunny weather brings out the desire to visit outdoor markets, and my sister had the inside scoop on a good one. This market covered a few acres and featured dozens of vendors selling everything from honey, to handcrafts, to machinery, and furniture. The guys combed through the tables filled with old tools while I found a bird's-eye maple ink blotter that I snatched up. (I love inkwells, pens, and blotters.)

An enterprising seamstress had created bins full of beautiful cushions that I longed to buy and take home. Alas, my luggage was already full so I consoled myself by remembering that I can actually make cushions with my own sewing machine if I really want/need them. It was a close one though.

Just look at those colours and fabrics, and all under a crabapple tree. My husband left empty handed (he's a man of few wants) but my brother-in-law found the perfect antique filing cabinet from a dealer he had met before.

The setting for the market was a field complete with flowers.

One of my favourite things about shopping in new places is not always what I can buy, but the ideas I get for making changes in my own house. The happy cushions gave me the idea to slip cover some of mine, to match the seasons. And a set of wrought iron gates made me wonder if they would work in my yard, along with a climbing rose, of course. So many ideas; so little luggage room.

After leaving the antiques market, and since we were in the neighbourhood, we went to visit the area where my Dewar relatives settled when they emigrated from Scotland in the early 1800s.

The town is called St. Andrews d'Argenteuil, or as it has been Francasized:, St. André-d'Argenteuil.

We took a tiny ferry (carrying only a dozen cars) across the Ottawa River and following GPS directions found the cemetery where our ancestors were buried. We have a copy of a geneology and history of the family, since before leaving Scotland for Canada, so we were able to locate the graves based on the names listed.

I know that graveyards are not fascinating to everyone but it was incredible being able to see the evidence of people in my family line who have lived and died. On the left is another ancestor's grave, and right, the grave marker of my great grandfather and his second wife, my great-grandmother, Eliza Jane.

Interestingly, the name Eliza was one that I considered for my first daughter. This was love before I knew that it was my great-grandmother's name. However, we ended up choosing a different name.

In Canada, Thanksgiving is always the second Monday in October. You might ask why it is so different from the date for Thanksgiving in the USA. I don't know the accurate answer to that other than different countries celebrate holidays on different dates. My theory is that harvest time is Canada is much earlier than in the US given our shorter growing season.

Happy Thanksgiving!

Dear Sweetie,

I remember exhibiting at a trade show many years ago and when the traffic through the show was slow, the exhibitors had a chance to chat with each other. One woman's name tag read, Victoria Lane. Since she sold lacy, Victorian-style products, it seemed like the perfect match. When I mentioned that, she smiled.

"You can call yourself whatever you want," she answered with a wink.

Another woman I know, when she signs up for mailing lists online, puts her name in as "Darling" because she decided she wanted to be called Darling more often. So today you get to be Sweetie, because who doesn't want to be called that?

The weather here has turned into the fall rains. According to my weather-watching husband, we've had 6 inches of rain over the past few days. Time to get out the rain boots again.

When I signed off last time, I was telling you about visiting my ancestors' graves in St. Andrews d'Argenteuil in Quebec. I am fascinated by old graveyards because they tell us so much about history. And about the value of life. Plus, they are usually pretty and peaceful, like this one.

When we cleaned out our parents' house in the spring, we came across several old albums containing photos from as far back as 1916. Among them was this photo of my great-grandparents, Donald and Eliza Jane Dewar. I was surprised to realize that Eliza Jane's eyes look just like my daughter's eyes how they slant at the corners. Isn't heredity fascinating?

In addition to pretty graveyards, there are also lovely old stone churches dotting the Quebec landscape. This one is the Rockburn Presbyterian church, which is near my sister's house.

This area of the province was settled predominantly by English-speaking people so many of the names and church denominations reflect that heritage. A short distance away, villages are more likely French and feature imposing churches with soaring spires. It's all such a lovely combination (though some Quebecers may not agree with me). People from many lands and nations have helped to build the Canada we know today and all have contributed value.

Apple Harvest

As I mentioned in my last letter, the area where we visited is an apple growing district and the trees were heavy with fruit. It's lovely to be able to eat apples from the trees just up the road, picked that morning. And so many varieties, some I have never heard of before, such as Ginger Gold, Lobo, Cortland, and Empire. I bought a mixed basket then when I went to eat them, couldn't remember which was which.

Of course, this necessitated another trip to the orchard store, where I had to also buy apple jelly.

Little surprises await at every turn. Tiny creeks meander through the landscape, gurgling over the rocks, such as this one, bordering the churchyard.

Stone houses, built in the 1800s, are still family homes, most surrounded by manicured, immaculate lawns.

One of my life goals is to visit every Canadian province and every US state. So, since we were so close to the border of New York state and Vermont, we decided to take a little jaunt across the line. I love exploring new places and I would be able to check off one more state on my list, now making it twenty-three that I've visited (I'd been to New York once before but just to cross the border at Niagara Falls).

Navigating with my cell phone and Google maps, we took back roads and scenic routes through farmlands, orchards, and skipping through the islands that are scattered through Lake Champlain. What fun!

"I haven't been everywhere, but it's on my list."
SUSAN SONTAG

This view is of Lake Champlain from one of the bridges that connect several islands. It's really lovely with lots to see. The road meanders past lush farms and through small towns.

Our destination was Burlington, though we hadn't set out to go there. It just seemed to be the next stop before heading back north.

The little river runs through Burlington and in the past it powered many mills along its banks.

Above, downtown Burlington, Vermont basks in the sun of a hot September day.

One of my favourite things to do is travel on backroads and see what we can see. Because there are so many trees in Quebec where we were visiting, it's hard to get a view unless you get up higher. (I'm all about the views.)

My sister owns an antique Morgan car, which is a blast to tour around in. We all hopped in the the open-topped car and found the highest point giving a clear view of Montreal, low mountains to the north, and a whole lot of trees.

One day on our meanderings we visited the charming covered Percy Bridge, built in 1861 and spanning a pretty little river.

Forests of sugar maples - the kind maple syrup comes from - are so big their foliage stretches right across the roads creating green tunnels.

This time of year it's apple season. Why not try a new apple dessert recipe like apple crisp or baked apples? Nothing says autumn like the scent of baking apples and cinnamon.

Until next time, stay happy!

Hello again.

As I write this, it's raining out—for the fourth time today. The first day of November dawns in shades of grey, which is not at all unusual. In fact, most days of November start this way. This is what I call the monsoon month here in the Pacific Northwest. From now until spring decides to arrive, clouds and rain will be the norm. Unless it snows...

As I've mentioned before (perhaps ad nauseum, I'm sorry), winter is not my favourite time of year. There is a reason for this. I don't like all the things that go with it, with the possible exception of snow on Christmas Eve that disappears by Boxing Day (December 26th).

I tend to be chilly. And I tend to suddenly overheat. So the up and down of the thermostat, and the subsequent on and off of the forced air from the furnace ensures that I'm rarely at a comfortable temperature.

I find bulky clothes uncomfortable and have since I was a young child. Being bundled up feels like trussed up to me, and wearing layers of clothing feels tight, heavy, and restrictive.

Additionally, I am also susceptible to Seasonal Affective Disorder, also known as SAD. At this latitude in the depths of winter, the sun (if it ever breaks through) gets over the mountains at around 10:00 AM, and it sets by 4:00 PM.

> ## Get plenty of fresh air and sunshine.
> — MOM

Seasonal affective disorder is caused by insufficient exposure to daylight and it saps your energy and lowers your mood, so being excited about anything is difficult. Thinking gets foggy, and concentrating is challenging. It's a good thing that I'm normally an upbeat person. I really work at not letting the dismal days get me down.

So what do you do in November when winter is approaching, or has already arrived, and you're not a fan of winter sports?

This isn't rocket science but if your goal is to get the most enjoyment you can out of November, there are some things you can do. Here are some of my favourites:

Plan something.

Happiness is often nothing more than having something to look forward to. If the view ahead seems bleak and the next several months promise more of the same, planning something fun or exciting can help dispel the blues.

If a winter vacation is possible, now is a good time to visit your local travel agent and pick up some of those glossy brochures with luscious photos of sundrenched beaches and turquoise water. Or start browsing online for destinations and travel deals. Join the mailing lists of airlines and resorts to be notified of upcoming specials.

Even if a sun destination isn't your cup of tea, lots of other locales can offer great off-season rates, and may include sipping a cup of tea by a roaring fire. Either way, planning a getaway makes winter more fun.

Now might be a great time to plan renovations or redecorating projects. Plan a new wardrobe, or design your garden, if you have one. Thinking about good things to come gives you something to look forward to.

> In the depth of winter I finally learned that there was in me an invincible summer.
> — ALBERT CAMUS

Start something.

Lots of classes and workshops gear up in the fall, so now is the time to take up a new pursuit. You don't have to enrol in a class to begin something new. Always wanted to learn to paint, or to write a book? Indoor days are the perfect time to hunker down and get started. If you learn to knit you could be wearing your new sweater or pair of hand-knit socks by the end of the month.

I learned to play the piano as a young person but seldom play it now. I find the oncoming winter months a great time to learn a new piece. Apparently, learning an instrument stimulates the brain, too. There's nothing wrong with that.

Starting a project by yourself or with someone else is a great way to spend the indoor months. What about a collection, a scrapbook, or re-finishing a piece of furniture? Stay occupied with something that gives you pleasure.

> I'm always interested in looking forward toward the future. Carving out new ways of looking at things.
> — TONY DANZA

Clear something.

This is a much better time for a closet clean out than spring. Once the tulips are blooming and the sun is shining, who wants to be stuck inside with her head in a dingy cupboard?

Cleaning and organizing, with its attendant chucking out of stuff I don't need/never use/doesn't fit, makes everything feel fresher and clearer. I keep a basket in a corner of my home office and whenever I come across something that no longer serves its purpose or is of use to me, it gets the heave-ho.

Naturally, trash and junk go straight into the garbage, but lots of things can be used and enjoyed by others in need of them. The items that make it into my box go to the local thrift store where they can bless someone else.

By the way, I'm not advocating for minimalist living, unless that's your wish. Personally, I like my stuff and want to keep it all, just in case I end up suddenly needing to use twelve metres of heavy red polyester fabric that I once bought for something, (long forgotten). But I've realized over the years, that I'm an out-of-sight-out-of-mind kind of person. Once I've given something away or tossed it out with the trash, I don't mourn its passing because I usually only vaguely remember ever owning it, if at all.

Finish something.

When I was sixteen I started embroidering a pair of pillowcases. I completely finished one of them, then I don't know...I got sidetracked, or too busy to finish embroidering the other one. I tucked them into a pretty round tin along with the embroidery hoop and some floss with the intention of completing the final work later.

Well, that tin with those pillowcases has been carted around to every one of my homes for over forty years. Every now and then I notice it in the top of the closet and think about getting it out and finishing it, then I close the closet door. Isn't it amazing how well and how long a person can put off finishing something? (Believe me, I'm not proud of this.) Since it is November, I think it might be time to just get it all out and finish the job, don't you?

While your UFOs (Unfinished Objects) might not have been hanging around in the back of a closet or a box under the bed as long as my pillow cases, I'm willing to guess that you've got a few more recent projects that need to be finished. Now as the days get shorter and life moves more indoors (at least it does in my neck of the woods), it would be a good time to get that project out and finish it. Imagine how great it will feel to finally get the thing done and off your "someday" list.

Do something.

I believe in choosing things in my life that please me and give me joy. Life is to be enjoyed after all. However, if my only goal is to please myself, I find that it begins to feel hollow fairly quickly. We're made to be part of community, however that looks, and to contribute to the lives of others so that life is better for all of us.

Few pursuits are more satisfying than doing something for the sake of someone else who needs you. Volunteering takes time so don't over stretch yourself if your plate is already full. If you're like me and working full time—and sometimes more than—there are other ways to contribute.

Find something that excites or interests you and see what there is in your community. Or contribute to a mission for needy people in other areas of the country or the world.

What I've learned from living through many Canadian winters is that when you look for joy and happiness, you'll find it. This applies to every part of life, of course, but particularly when you feel like you're sinking emotionally.

Remember, happiness is nothing more than having something to look forward to. Now, curl up with a hot drink, something yummy to eat, and a good book. Enjoy November.

love Wendy

Hi All,

This letter is a little different given the upcoming season. Already we've had snow here and the surrounding mountains look beautiful. There is also a cold wind outside, but let's not talk about that right now.

For the record I want to say right now that I am not an early Christmas decorator. I am not one of those people who the minute the last trick or treater tottered her little sugar-stuffed, princess-costumed body down my front steps I start hauling the Christmas decorations out of the back closet.

On the other hand, if I don't plan I know I'll be stressed out at some point along the journey to Bethlehem's big celebration and am of an age now (never mind) that I don't want stress to be part of my life any more.

I've spent a lot of years awake at night with my mind caught up in the trap of anxiety and stress over stuff I've long since forgotten about. I'm done doing that. I like a slow pace and preparing for what's coming up helps a lot.

So in the interest of making the upcoming holiday season easy and more relaxed for all of us, I've created a six-week planning checklist so you don't have to make your own list, or try to keep all these details in your head. I want you to have a stress-free holiday season too.

Now just because something is on this list doesn't mean you have to do it.

I stopped sending out Christmas cards about five years ago and have never regretted it. I still get lots of cards and love receiving them, and people tell me they love sending them. In that case the exercise makes two people happy. For me, having another job to do didn't make me happy; it simply made me more stressed out. So I stopped.

I'm all about keeping things quick and simple so that we can spend time on what gives us joy, happiness, and more fun. Are you with me?

Here goes...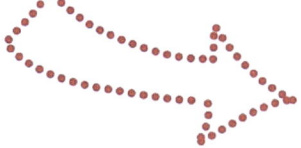

Six weeks before December 25th

Order Christmas cards, or if you do family photo cards, now is the time to have the photos taken or processed.

Making gifts this year? Check your supply list and stock up on what you will need.

Buy gift wrap, gift bags and ribbon. But first, check if you have any on hand from last year. (I always buy way too much and have stock piles from years ago that never got used up.)

Decide on your spending budget for everything, and also for categories such as gifts, entertaining, meals, and incidentals, like coffee with friends.

Five weeks before December 25th

Create a calendar for everything you need to do and when. Include social engagements, activities, and commitments. Be sure to include the activities these events require to prepare, too.

Check your stings of lights for dead bulbs. Replacement bulbs sell out fast, so don't wait until the last minute.

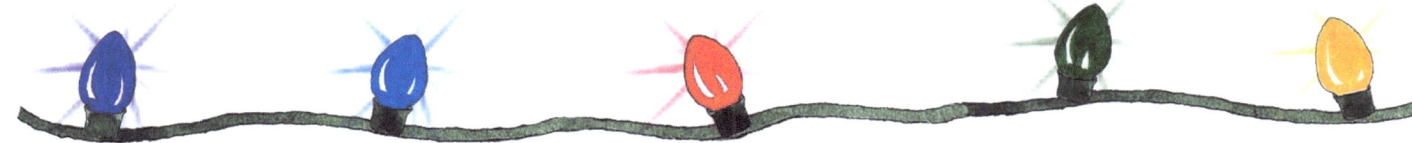

Four weeks before Christmas

Hang your Christmas wreath on the front door and put up your outdoor lights.

Start, and hopefully finish, your gift shopping. Be sure to shop with a list rather than wandering the stores looking for ideas. You'll save lots of time, and money, if you shop prepared.

This is the time to mail out your Christmas cards. Start your Advent calendar.

Watch a Christmas movie, or six.
Have coffee with a friend.
Buy a book to read over the holidays.
Take a soothing bath, or get a massage.

Three weeks before Christmas

Put up your Christmas tree. Actually, you can do this whenever it works for you.

Some folks want the tree up right after Halloween, others wait until Christmas eve.

I generally opt for a couple of weeks before Christmas because I once had a baby on December 11th. I would put the tree up around the 10th, cover it with balloons, and call it the birthday tree.

After the birthday, the balloons came down and the Christmas decorations went up.

Deck the halls with boughs of whatever you have for decor.

Start your Christmas baking—or buying.

Plan the menus for family dinners, or holiday entertaining.

Check the gift shopping list and pick up any stocking stuffers or hostess gifts.

Stay within your budget and don't be swayed by sparkle and shine advertising.

Two weeks before Christmas

Clean out the refridgerator to make room for lots of dishes and treats.

Clean the house from top to bottom, prepare guest rooms, put out towels. If you're going away, you can skip this step. Yay!

Even if you're not having guests for the holidays, it's nice to have a clean house as it lessens your stress levels.

Do the minimum you need to do to feel relaxed.

Go for a drive and look at the lights. End the evening with a mug of hot chocolate.

One week before Christmas

Arrange the features of your Christmas table and get everything ready to set it on the big day. Order your fresh centrepiece or purchase candles.

Grocery shop for Christmas Eve, Christmas dinner, and other entertaining needs.

Keep everything as simple and easy as you can. The goal is to keep stress at bay and enjoy yourself.

Wrap last minute gifts.

Put on the Christmas music and put your feet up.

Prepare any make-ahead dishes and food gifts.

Go out for coffee with a friend or family member. Call your mom, if you can.

The last few days before December 25th

If you don't want to do any of these suggestions, just don't do them.

Remember the reason for the celebration is the birth of a Saviour who came into the world amongst songs of peace on earth.

If something doesn't give you peace, chances are it gives you stress. By recognizing what gives you peace versus what stresses you out, you can make choices that will give you the most enjoyment of the season.

Wendy

Dear One,

Winter arrives as softly as kittens' feet on a sheepskin rug. The snow drifts down from the night sky, illuminated in the lights of the town, fat flakes catching in tree branches and resting silently on evergreen boughs.

It is as December should be in this part of the world. No -40 degree temperatures. No raging blizzards that stop traffic, close schools, and take out power lines. Just a beautiful, gentle snowfall. Tomorrow it will stop, or maybe not.

The snow piles up, the plow roars by early the next morning, pushing the accumulated white stuff up into heaps and mounds. Oh, to be a child when there is suddenly a snow mountain just down the street.

Snowflakes are kisses from heaven.

Of course, it doesn't always happen this way, as romantic as it sounds. Sometimes what we get is grey skies and unceasing rain, gloomy and dark for weeks, as the shortest day of the year looms closer. When that happens, the sun, if we even get a glimpse of it, has disappeared by four o'clock.

We all know that December isn't just about the weather, even though it can be intrusive at times. December is the month of Christmas and everything that goes with it: parties, family events, shopping and much more.

A few years ago, while I was involved in a lot more social and business organizations than I am now, I attended ten different Christmas parties in the first couple of weeks of the month. I love a good turkey dinner but by about the eighth one, I had tasted every variation of stuffing that I wanted to. It actually began to be comical. By the time Christmas day arrived, I was once again ready to cook up another turkey dinner and share it with my family. So delectable!

> "O, wind, if winter comes, can spring be far behind?"
>
> PERCY BYSSHE SHELLEY

In my last letter, I suggested plans you can follow to help make your holiday time more organized, and hopefully less stressful. As I paid for my own shopping one day this month, the cashier at the store shared with me that she didn't find the holidays much fun. With three young children at home, while she wanted to provide a lovely time for her family, for her it was all just so much work.

Over the years, I've pared down what I do to "put on" Christmas. My children have long-since left the nest, so when I haul out the decorations from storage, I find myself wanting to keep things simpler. Sometimes the enjoyment is more in the having done it than in the actual doing of it. For example, I love to have a pretty tree with all the lights and ornaments I can fit on it, but having a simpler version and more time to sit in its glow and read a book make the time more peaceful.

Some people thrive on activity and action, and there are times when I do too. Activity without purpose, though, is not fulfilling and ends up being draining and even exhausting. Resentment may even follow. We don't want that.

The key to keeping the joy and happiness in the season, even while everything ramps up toward the holidays, is to know your priorities and stick to what matters.

Here are a few questions to ask before committing to anything this month:

Do I care about this enough to spend my precious time on it?

So often we do things the same way we've always done them, out of habit, or not wanting to rock anyone's boat. But it's important to understand why you do something, not just that you have to do it. If the joy or the purpose no longer exists, perhaps it's time to start a new tradition. New traditions breathe new life into special events and it is not difficult to do. Ideas are everywhere.

By living your life seeking the joy, your purpose is never in question. Being more joyful in your own life spreads the joy around you. Every action can be prefaced with the question: How can I make this more joyful?

It's so easy to have a furrowed brow (which causes wrinkles, by the way) when faced with a massive to-do list. But the person who made the list can also make a new list in which the goal is more joy.

A story to remember

Many, many years ago a young woman, heavily pregnant, rode into a faraway town on a donkey. Everything was bustling and all accommodations were overfull. If you've ever given birth, I'm sure you can only imagine how uncomfortable being in labour while riding on the back of a burro would feel.

And it came to pass in those days...

The night was dark and cold, and the young woman's husband led the donkey with his suffering bride from inn to inn and found nowhere for them to rest. The baby was due to be born any moment; perhaps her water had already broken. Finally, a kind innkeeper sized up their situation and offered the only thing he could—a place in the barn.

Barns are generally heated only by the bodies of the animals inside. This one was likely no exception. That cold night, unbeknownst to a town full of people intent on their own business, and a world that slept in ignorance, the saviour of the human race was born. It happened in a dark stone barn, on a quiet night, unnoticed by an entire city.

Yet the event was so momentous that angels lit up the skies out on the hills where shepherds gathered close around a small fire, warming their hands and glancing over their shoulders to keep their sheep safe from predators. Imagine their utter shock and dismay when an entire heavenly host appeared before their eyes and announced the news.

It was so momentous that a dazzling star lit up the sky and half a world away astronomers and seekers of wisdom gathered their caravans and left their homelands to follow where it led.

The people of the nation where the birth took place had no idea that this humble event would change the course of history, and this child would live and die, then rise from the dead, to wipe away the barriers between mankind and a loving God.

God is crazy-in-love with people, all people. He prepared heaven for us when our time here on earth is done. But only perfect people can be in God's presence, and God knows, none of us is perfect. So how can we experience heaven? On our own, it is impossible. Only divine intervention can wipe our slates clean.

Jesus was born to pay the price for our imperfection. He took all our sin on himself and did it willingly when he died in our place. How can we know God, and be completely clean and totally guilt-free?

Believe in me, is what Jesus says. "Anyone who believes in me won't perish, but will have everlasting life." It' seems too good to be true, but it is the best transaction ever offered in the history of the world. "Believe in me..." It's so simple and it's far too good to pass up. The life of faith in Jesus Christ is the most exciting, rewarding life imaginable. I know from experience, the gospel is good news.

I hope that this season brings you joy, happiness, and the peace of which the angels sang. As the month draws to a close and another year winds down, I wish you good health, prosperity, and so much love that you won't be able to contain it and it will spill over to everyone around you.

John 3:16

With much love and many blessings,

Wendy

Acknowledgements

Many people played a part in the creation of this book, though most may not know it. Most of the letters were written during a particularly difficult year that began with the death of my mother. I am grateful to those who subscribed to The Letter Box and gave me such lovely feedback.

I'm thankful for my parents and that I was raised to know the Lord Jesus in a personal way. There is no substitute for His grace and salvation in my life.

My husband, Gord, has given me the gift of believing in my abilities, even when things haven't worked out as hoped, which has been more often than we both care to remember.

My daughters provide me with endless happiness and knowing them keeps me looking forward to new adventures. My grandchildren are a new delight in my life.

To my friend and creative buddy, author and coach, Suzanne Lieurance, thanks for keeping me on track every week when I've wanted to take off after another new idea.

How to find me:

Websites
www.wendydewarhughes.com
www.summerbaystudio.com
inlovewithfrance.com

My books
Amazon and Kindle
IBookstore
Kobo, Barnes and Noble, and more

Design Products
Amazon
Etsy
EBay

Illustrated Books by Wendy Dewar Hughes

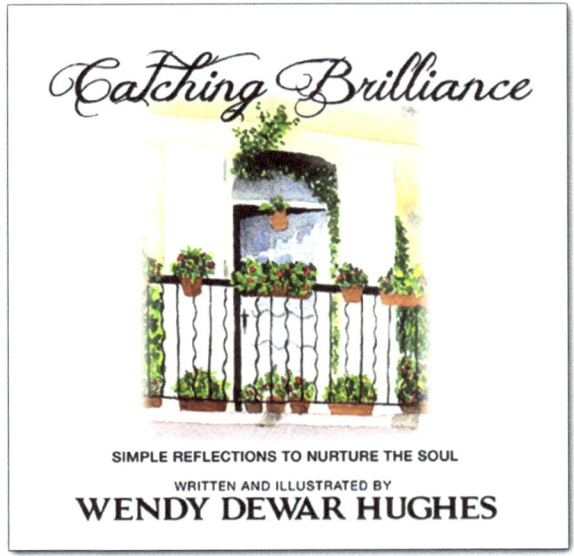

Available online in Print

www.wwendydewarhughes.com

Journals by Wendy Dewar Hughes

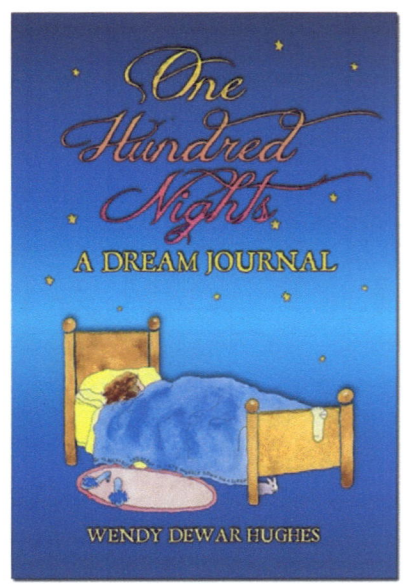

Available online in Print

www.wendydewarhughes.com

Fiction by Wendy Dewar Hughes

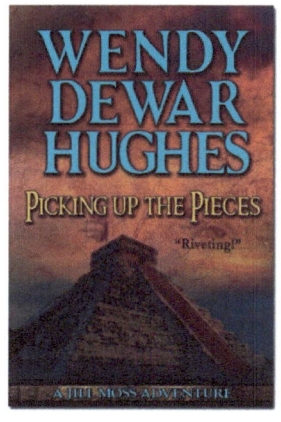
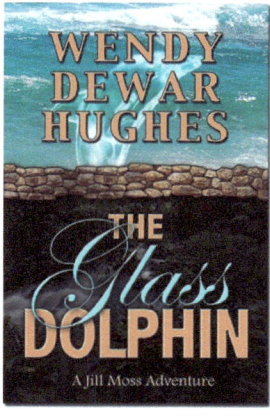

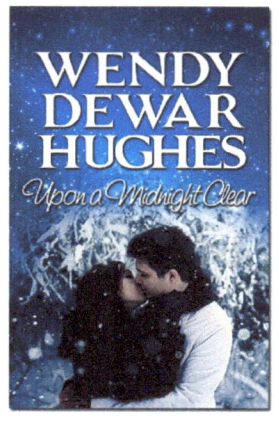
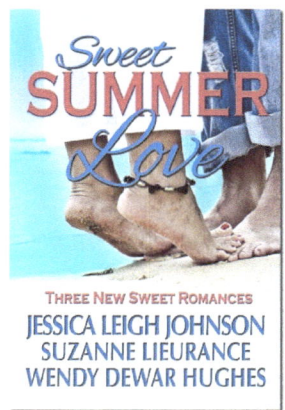

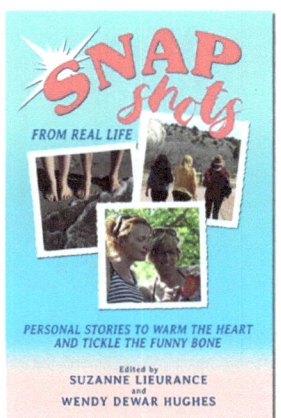

Available online in Print and E-Book
www.wendydewarhughes.com

www.ingramcontent.com/pod-product-compliance
Lightning Source LLC
Chambersburg PA
CBHW042005150426
43194CB00003B/135